WHA‍T‍   ‍E?

OLDCASTLE BOOKS

Leon Marc is a diplomat and writer, with a deep interest in history. Currently the Slovenian Ambassador to the Netherlands, he studied Public Policy and Management in the UK and was involved in the student movement in his native country at the time of the fall of the Berlin Wall. He witnessed his country joining the European Union in 2004 as a diplomat in Dublin, and later dealt with the Western Balkans file. He is married to Barbara Blaznik and they have one daughter.

WHAT'S *SO* EASTERN

ABOUT

EASTERN EUROPE?

TWENTY YEARS AFTER THE FALL OF THE BERLIN WALL

LEON MARC

OLDCASTLE BOOKS

First published in 2009 by Oldcastle Books
PO Box 394, Harpenden, Herts, AL5 1XJ
www.oldcastlebooks.com

The views expressed in this book are the author's and do not necessarily express the views of the organisation where he is employed.

Editor Nick Rennison

A CIP catalogue record for this book is available from the British Library.

ISBN 978-1-84243-340-9

2 4 6 8 10 9 7 5 3 1

Printed and bound in Great Britain by
CPI Antony Rowe, Chippenham and Eastbourne

To the memory of Drago (Karl) Lavrenčič

ACKNOWLEDGEMENTS

If there was ever somebody to (unconsciously and indirectly) inspire the writing of this book, this was certainly Drago (Karl) Lavrenčič – a man to whose memory I dedicate this book and with whom this book also begins. He was the one who taught me – among many other things – to appreciate the phenomenon of Central Europe. I am deeply indebted to him.

During my years in Ireland, where I got the idea for this book, another man greatly influenced my thinking. After he was almost accidentally dispatched to Slovenia in a group of wine experts, Enda O'Doherty developed a great interest in the country and perhaps even fell in love with it. Together we grew the habit of meeting at the café of the French Cultural Centre in Dublin to debate current affairs, history and books. He was also the first to see the early version of the manuscript of this book and to give a critical and valuable assessment. I am grateful for his continued friendship over the years.

Thanks also to Prof Jaap de Zwaan for his kind words on the manuscript. Ion Mills at Oldcastle Books was the man who recognised the value of this text and dared to publish it. It was a pleasure working with him. I also wish to acknowledge the great help of Claire Watts, also at Oldcastle Books, for her dedicated work on the book. My thanks go to the language editor, Nick Rennison too, who polished my non-native English.

My wife Barbara offered generous support to my ambitions as an author – I hope these did not compromise too much my ambitions as husband and father! As for the latter, it will be many years before our daughter Metka Brigita will have grown up to be able to read this book, but I hope that she will appreciate it too.

CONTENTS

Preface: The End of a Divided Europe

In *What's So Eastern About Eastern Europe*, Leon Marc has written a very personal account of the political, economic and social history of the countries of Central and Eastern Europe. It is a complete, comprehensive and concise study but its central thesis is that unfortunate stereotypes about Eastern Europe continue to exist in Western Europe.

Marc establishes that, notwithstanding the accession of twelve states of Central and Eastern Europe to the European Union in 2004 and 2007, in the eyes of Western Europeans, there is still a division in the continent between West and East. Marc strongly argues the case against this perception, although he agrees that, over the centuries, the peoples of Eastern Europe, when compared with their fellow citizens in Western Europe, have had different experiences of some of the continent's major historical and social developments. He cites the schism between the Western and Eastern Roman churches; the fall of Rome in Western Europe parallel to the rise of Byzantium in Eastern Europe; the siege of Constantinople in 1453 by the Turks; the presence of the Ottoman Empire in the Eastern part of our continent for several centuries; and, with particular reference to recent history, the 40-year-long Cold War which followed the long period of extremely violent conflict on the European continent that included the First and Second World Wars. In examining the latter period, the author reminds us of the sufferings of the Eastern European peoples under a Communist rule which was imposed on them against their will.

Marc rightly explains the extent to which Eastern Europe has contributed to the variety and richness of European history and culture – indeed, to European civilization as a whole. His book refers to the pioneering work of Cyril and Methodius, the two preachers from Greece who came to Western Europe to bring Christianity; the role Eastern European peoples played in bringing the Ottoman (and Mongol) presence on our continent to an end and, within living memory, the resistance of many individuals in the countries of Central and Eastern Europe to Communism. His analysis results in the (obviously correct) conclusion that Western and Eastern Europe have shared a common history over the centuries and today they share so many beliefs and values that they must be considered two parts of one single civilization. There is no justification in making further distinctions between the Eastern and Western halves of the continent.

In his analysis Leon Marc also pays attention to the position of his own country, Slovenia. In a subtle manner he reminds us that Slovenia, although formally part of Eastern Europe, has so many characteristics of its own. The country is located next to Italy, developed strong ties with Austria over the centuries (with the Habsburg Monarchy to be more precise) and never belonged to the area often referred to as the Western Balkans. Furthermore Slovenia, during a membership which only started in 2004, has adapted itself in a very short, indeed record, time to the standards and values of the European Union. The successful introduction of the single EU currency, the Euro, in 2007, for example, represents an extraordinary achievement for the country.

The publication of Leon Marc's book is well timed. Indeed, it seems that today many citizens in Western Europe are not sufficiently aware of the existence of the other part of our continent, nor of the significance it has had in shaping our common history and culture. On the contrary, a glance at recent history establishes that the recent enlargements of the EU to the East and the consequent concerns Western European citizens have expressed about immigration to their countries from the new member states, have had a negative impact on the outcome of the French and Dutch referenda on the Constitutional Treaty in 2005 and on the Irish vote on the Lisbon Treaty in 2008. Such results show that many people in Western Europe do not know their history. They also demonstrate that the peoples of Europe do not know each other well enough. This situation has to change. There are so many reasons we should get to know our Eastern neighbours better. Without exception, all the new member states can boast beautiful cities, full of Gothic, Renaissance, Baroque and Rococo buildings and monuments. They can point to their wonderful countryside and landscapes. Perhaps some of their languages are difficult to understand but these languages also represent an enrichment of our general European culture. More face-to-face contacts between the peoples of the West and those of the East must be encouraged. In the realms of education, research and culture, great strides can be made towards improving relations between all European peoples.

Unfortunately, the financial and economic crises in Europe, in the last year, have revealed more clearly certain differences in development between the new member states and the older ones. It seems that, because several of the new member states have not yet completed their economic reforms, stumbling blocks to economic development in the new Europe have emerged. We should not allow this to happen. Solidarity between West and East should prevail.

The Cold War is over, the Iron Curtain has been lifted; the division in Europe has ended. As a result, we have created an ever-growing space of peace, stability and prosperity on our continent. In parallel with that, an internal market – an area without internal frontiers in which the free movement of persons, goods, services and capital is ensured – has emerged. Let's profit fully from all of the opportunities this new situation can offer us.

The arrival of Leon Marc's book is also well timed because, in 2009, we celebrate the twentieth anniversary of the fall of the Berlin Wall. What better moment for us all to realise that Europe is one continent which shares the same commitment to human rights, parliamentary democracy, independent judiciary and good governance. The fact that our continent has a variety of religions

13

does not alter this conclusion. In fact, there are historical reasons for the presence in Europe of other traditions than the Christian and Jewish ones. In recent times, the processes of globalisation and internationalisation may have led to an increase in this presence but, the creation of a multicultural society in Europe, can be looked at as an enrichment of our civilization.

The future will bring us many challenges and opportunities. In the interest of securing values like peace and stability in Europe (and beyond) we must do our utmost to develop good relations with our neighbouring countries, Russia included. The existence of such a relationship between the EU and Russia may, for example, bring (more) stability to the Caucasus, both the northern part and the southern part. Similarly, the accession of Turkey to the European Union can have a positive impact on that area. EU concepts such as 'Eastern partnership' and the model of the 'Partnership and Cooperation Agreement' can be some of the means by which a more stable situation can be encouraged. The strengthening of bilateral contacts can also contribute to the creation of more stability and, hopefully, prosperity in our part of the world.

Comprehensively and concisely, Leon Marc's book presents readers with vital insights into the different dimensions of our common European history and culture. What makes reading his book all the more enjoyable is that he does so with his own personal touch. The book can and should be read by everybody – by all Europeans but especially by those of us who live in the (Western) countries that are the oldest member states of the European Union.

Prof Dr Jaap W. de Zwaan, Director of the Nederlands Institute of International Relations, Clingendael, in The Hague, the Netherlands

Prologue: The Three Classmates

In late July 2003, I stood in a funeral home near Cobham in Surrey, paying my last respects to a man called Karl Lavrenčič. As the coffin was quietly sliding into the mouth of the crematorium, I was overwhelmed by my emotions. In this English suburb the slightly insecure voices of an amateur male group, singing traditional Slovenian funeral hymns, were something from another world. Watching his family and friends, and the Slovenian Catholic priest from London who was conducting the service, the thought slipped through my mind that this man died in the wrong place. Despite all that Karl did for his native country, it was his dying in England – the country that had long ago become his new and (most probably) truest home – that really gave the impression that he had been finally and forever lost to his fatherland.

Karl Lavrenčič[1] and his wife Dora were very good to me. I do not recall exactly how I first met him. It must have been on one of his trips to Slovenia. Formally retired, he continued his freelance work for the Economist Intelligence Unit, for the Slovenian Section of the BBC and for other organisations. His work meant everything to him. Once he lost his wallet at Waterloo Station but managed to retrieve it at the lost & found desk. He gave the surprised student, who found the purse, a very, very generous reward. But, as he was telling us later, he was not concerned about the cash or the credit cards: he was concerned about his BBC pass. 'Imagine, Dora,' he said to his wife, 'all the fuss I would have had to endure had I not found the wallet with my BBC pass in it.'

Every morning, there were papers from all over the world waiting on the doorstep of his home in Oxshott. And despite his age – he

---

[1]More about his life at
http://findarticles.com/p/articles/mi_qn4158/is_20030728/ai_n12711675

was over 70 at the time – he still used to travel around the globe. Annual IMF and World Bank gatherings in Washington were his staple food, as were monthly trips to Slovenia. There, he walked into my office one day at one of the newly-emerged political parties, where I was in charge of international affairs. From then on, we kept in touch, and I was a welcome visitor to his and Dora's home. During my studies at the University of London, I often spent weeks there preparing for the exams.

He and Dora lived a very comfortable life by the time they both retired. But it was not always like that. Karl came to the UK with little more than the clothes he stood up in. Dora, the daughter of a senior Slovenian national politician from the years before the Second World War, did not fare much better. She came from a wealthy and respected conservative family of Slovenian patriots; he was the son of a liberal father, a former Austrian imperial teacher, and an ethnic-German mother. He managed to survive the Second World War but he was unhappy about the kind of liberty that Yugoslav Communists were able to deliver and, after a brief spell in prison, he fled the country. With his gift for languages he made his way through the displaced persons' camp in Austria to the UK. There he went through a number of jobs before he managed to settle at the BBC Slovenian service, finished a degree in economics (to add to the one in law he brought with him from home), and began what was to be a remarkable career in journalism. He toured the Communist world (described in *Living with Communism*, published in 1966 under the pseudonym of Anthony Silvester), but then he dedicated himself to Africa, which he knew inside out. Yet he never lost interest in Yugoslavia and Slovenia.

Karl was a law student, with a great interest in economics and international affairs when World War Two started. Two of his classmates at Ljubljana University at the time were men whose lives would continue to be intertwined with his in the future – Ljubo Sirc, the son of a wealthy businessman, and Aleksander Bajt, a former altar boy. Ljubo too ended up in the UK soon after the war, where he worked his way up to become a university professor in Glasgow. Another liberal but also a Yugoslav patriot, he was at first a firm believer in the idea of Tito's resistance movement which he joined. Yet this did not spare his father a death sentence following a notorious show trial soon after the Communists came to power and he himself narrowly escaped the same fate. Years later, he established in London the Centre for Research into Communist Economies, an academic think-tank researching the Communist economic experiment at a time when not many Western academics seriously thought that this experiment had something to offer. Ljubo wanted to prove the opposite.

Aleksander Bajt followed a different path. He came from a deeply religious family and both Ljubo and Karl would later recall that he had been a very pious young man. So Karl was enormously surprised when, one morning after the war, he bumped into Aleksander, wearing the *partisan* uniform with the red star on his hat, and speaking passionately about the new world order that was being established in the country. According to Karl's later accounts, this meeting finally convinced Karl to leave the new Yugoslavia. Or, as he put it in his book, he left because he was 'unable to enjoy life in a closely regimented society'.

But Aleksander's story does not end there. He too had a great interest in economics. In fact, his red star helped him to make a career that he had probably never even dreamed about. Not only did he establish a university career in his native country during the Communist era, but he was also able to found and run a relatively autonomous economics institute in Ljubljana, the Slovenian capital. As the Yugoslav and, in particular, the Slovenian socialist economy was flirting with the logic of capitalist economy; his institute grew in fame and was usually referred to simply as 'Bajt's institute'. And while he always remained within the boundaries of the official economic ideology, he was also allowed opportunities to set the limits of what that ideology should be. But that was all: he never crossed them, at least not until his very last years. His book, *Berman's Dossier* (written in Slovenian), was a bulky volume of a thousand-plus pages which few read in its entirety and it was completed almost literally on his deathbed. It shook many in Slovenia. By then, books critical of the Communist system were not that rare anymore. But it was shocking that Bajt, a respected scientist and a former partisan comrade himself, should present an utterly revisionist and devastatingly critical account of the partisan resistance and revolutionary movement, shaking the foundations of what the nation had learnt about the Second World War. This was no longer the man with a hat with a red star.

Ljubo too got involved. With his eternal, almost naïve belief (as many saw it) in the intrinsic good of mankind, he accepted the challenge offered by a new political party (born out of the Socialist Youth Organisation that now re-branded itself as the Liberal Democratic Party) and decided to run for President of Slovenia about the time that Bajt's book came out. He did not come even close to winning and Ljubo, so he said later, concluded that he had been used as a liberal figurehead by men who did not exactly share his passionate and deep belief in liberalism. (His legal battle for the restitution of the family-owned business, which was nationalised after World War Two, is even today only partially solved.)

Karl stayed away from politics all his life. He could never have accepted the role that Bajt played for so many years, tacitly approving of the Communist regime. Nor would he ever have dared to believe in a bunch of young men who called themselves Liberals. He was too cautious, too sceptical and too pragmatic for any of these roles. For all his life he was an observer, although a very thorough and objective one. This was recognised by many reputable institutions that sought his advice or commissioned his reports.

Each of the three classmates could tell his own personal story about Eastern Europe as they knew it. Two of them – like so many from all over Eastern Europe – fled their native country. One, despite his very different upbringing, stayed on and fully integrated himself into Communist society. He didn't speak up until the end of his life. Karl kept coming to Yugoslavia all his life. Ljubo never stopped hoping for a change. Karl used the power of radio and as a result Aleksander's voice was heard from his deathbed.

Their stories are all equally fascinating. Ljubo was sentenced to death, but then pardoned. (Despite this, he is still one of the warmest and good-humoured people I have ever met.) Aleksander enjoyed a peaceful life in his native country. Karl had the experience of the exile too. Both Karl and Ljubo started from nothing and worked their way up the ladder in a country that was not exactly in need of highly-educated refugees from Yugoslavia.

Thinking of this as Karl was laid to rest in the middle of the English countryside, a thousand miles away from the baroque beauties of his native Ljubljana, from the Julian Alps and the vast forests that lie at their feet, I thought that his story – and those of his two classmates – needed to be told and explained. The local English priest, who was present at the ceremony, watched and listened to the Slovenian hymns with respect, but with a hint of puzzlement in his eyes. Who, after all, was this man he seemed to be asking. Where did he come from? What do I know of his country and why is he being laid in his grave here? The Berlin Wall has been down for some time – a full twenty years, in fact – and yet there is scope to explain why it was built in the first place and who the people were who were left on the other side, in the East.

Introduction: Eastern Europeans Descend on the Isles

Ruairi seemed rather lonely. In the Superquinn supermarket, in a wealthy Dublin suburb on a Saturday morning, he was one of the few Irish staff at the checkout. The girl serving us was from Lithuania, and my wife and I were also from what is described as Eastern Europe. The night before, we had had dinner in a Lebanese restaurant with a Slovakian couple. The two waitresses were Polish and the belly dancer was German, presumably former East German.

From Dublin to the north-western county of Donegal, Eastern Europeans have settled into Ireland. From May 2004, the day of the EU accession of eight new member states to the end of 2007, more than 265,000[2] people from Poland alone came to seek work in Ireland (including dependents and those that may have already left Ireland in the meantime). Although the current recession in Ireland has reduced (possibly even stopped) the inflow, the number of those actually working in Ireland as I write is still high. The decision of the Irish Government in 2004 to end the system of work-permits for workers from new member states was hailed by the opposition, business and trade unions alike, as an important step forward. It was seen as a way of securing much-needed working hands for the Celtic Tiger – and also perhaps as a means of avoiding a potentially much more troublesome immigration from outside of the EU.

Apart from Ireland, only the UK opened its labour market equally generously in 2004. In the period from May 2004 to March 2007, some 630,000 people from the eight accession states sought work in the UK[3]. This may seem a lot but, in proportion to the population, the figures for Ireland are even more impressive. Furthermore, the UK has for some time been a desired destination for foreign job seekers, and has traditionally been (at least in the cities) a

---

[2] See http://www.welfare.ie/topics/ppsn/ppsstat.html#euten040506
[3] Accession Monitoring Report, A8 Countries, May 2004 – March 2007, Home Office, May 2007

multicultural society, so a couple of hundred thousand Eastern Europeans should not have represented a major challenge. (At least this is what most people thought.) The Irish experience, however, has been quite different. Immigration there is a quite recent phenomenon and has come only a generation (or less) after Ireland began to recover from its own brain- and youth-drain. It is (or was) taking place in a society that is not really used to foreigners but also in one that – as I will try to show later on – shares a number of features with the societies of Eastern Europe.

It does not, therefore, come as a great surprise that Ireland (even before the recession hit the world) soon became perplexed about whether it was indeed a good idea to have workers from the new member states allowed in without work-permits. Until recently there was a general consensus that they have been a good thing for the Irish economy: they have mostly taken jobs as construction workers, grocery shop assistants, or waiters and maids – jobs that are usually not particularly attractive to the 'natives'. But, following some controversial cases, people began to wonder if workers from so-called Eastern Europe were indeed taking Irish jobs – despite the continued decline in unemployment. An opposition leader challenged the Government on the issue of childcare allowance being paid to the children of the workers from new EU member states and the representative of the National Safety Council of Ireland publicly attributed the increase in road-deaths to the drink-driving culture of Eastern Europeans and the allegedly poor standards of driving schools in the new EU member states.

Whatever the differences between the two driving (and drinking) cultures, because I lived in Ireland for four years, it became obvious to me (even before large numbers of Eastern Europeans set foot on Irish shores) that the lack of understanding of Eastern Europe and Eastern Europeans was becoming an issue. For centuries, Ireland used to be a country of emigration. 'Nobody ever wanted to come here', the Irish say. On the contrary, people just did not know how to get out quickly enough. The sight of so many now so eager to enter the country is a source of both puzzlement and pride to the Irish. Yet even now, despite the talk of multiculturalism, Ireland is not yet fully used to foreigners of any nationality, except perhaps the British. And Eastern Europeans represent the most recent, the most numerous and, with the exception of non-Europeans, allegedly the most difficult challenge.

But even those – and they are the majority in Ireland – who do respect the dignity of immigrants, sometimes speak about workers from Eastern Europe as if they were from an entirely different culture and required nothing less than an introduction to the ways of Europe. Of course, immigrants of all nationalities and times have always been a very diverse group, ranging from the most alien to the most adaptable, from the brightest and the most able, who simply could not find a job to match their abilities at home, to the poorest and least skilled, who have nothing to lose from travelling abroad in search of work. And, yes, there are even those who see a foreign country as a place for more sinister, perhaps illegal, opportunities. (Even, perhaps, reckless driving on treacherous Irish roads!) Eastern Europeans too come in all shapes and forms.

The issue of 'Eastern Europeans' in Ireland prompted me to start thinking about what it is that makes me feel European and why I am not comfortable with the label Eastern European, at least not when it is used, as it so often is, to imply a *Lesser* European. In fact, I have often felt like I woke up to a new world in 1990, when people in Western Europe started to call us by this uninspiring name – Eastern Europeans. As a famous Slovenian writer commented, Eastern Europe was created (again) with the European Enlargement Day of 2004. And the more we keep saying that this is not our name, the more it seems to be used.

The vast majority of Irish are genuinely welcoming and open people. Continentals and, even more so, Eastern Europeans, with their experience of Communism, are much more wary and watchful. (I will try to explain this later.) On the other hand, lack of knowledge of the Continent, and of Eastern Europe in particular, is not helpful when trying to understand Eastern Europeans on a temporary visit to Irish or English shores. Many of the older generation of Irish simply spoke of the whole of Eastern Europe as of 'Russia' – it was an alien, pagan and wrecked land. (On one occasion in 1958, when the Yugoslav regime put a Croatian Catholic bishop on trial, the bishop of Dublin warned the faithful against attending a scheduled football match against a team from Communist Yugoslavia – with little effect though.) The new generations do not always seem to have advanced all that much, since their ventures into the Continent are too often limited to sunny *playa* and cheap booze in one of the Eastern European capitals. The Irish, of course, are not alone in their attitudes. I have met many (too many) Italians who were not aware that their country has a common border with Slovenia, and low-cost airline stag-party trips of young Brits to Bratislava or Ljubljana are not exactly signs of an enlightened search for the truth about Eastern Europe. Even closer to Eastern Europe, in Germany, the younger generation have lost all notion of the long-established links between the German-speaking world and the Slavs (an interaction to which I devote an entire chapter) that so much characterised the history of Europe. And in the Netherlands, the country where I live and work now, Eastern Europeans – including diplomats – are struggling hard to shake off all the negative stereotypes associated with the lands beyond the invisible *new* Berlin Wall.

Soon after my arrival in The Hague, I contacted a Dutch business, wholly owned by a Slovenian company. Their product, originally designed in Slovenia, has a strong brand name here, and is seen every day on the streets of the Netherlands. I wanted to have it displayed on the Slovenian stand at a business conference, both to illustrate the close connections between the two economies, and to prove that sometimes it is Eastern Europe that invests in and sells knowledge to the West. The otherwise friendly manager refused to send the product to the conference, as he thought that knowing it came from Eastern Europe (or perhaps even the Balkans) would negatively affect his sales in the Netherlands.

This book came out of the belief that so-called Western Europeans need some introduction to Eastern Europe too. Because I was living in Ireland at the time of the historical 2004 enlargement of the EU, it could not avoid something of an Irish flavour (and, indeed, I added this with great pleasure) but other 'Western Europeans' are, in my view, and as evidenced by my Dutch experience, just as much in need of an introduction to Eastern Europe. My aim here is to explain what Eastern Europe was and what it is today; how it came to be known as Eastern Europe and why this name is increasingly misleading. This is not a scientific treatise or a history book, although I very much hope that nothing in it contradicts historical facts: I draw extensively on well-known historic events, described in the appendices at the end of the book (the vast majority of literature used was published in English). History is unavoidable if one tries to explain why Eastern Europe is and always has been an essential part of Europe.

This book is also meant to be a popular read. I am certainly not putting forward many new facts but I am offering new interpretations of known ones. Of course, each interpretation involves a certain simplification – and I am aware of that – but so little of the literature on Eastern Europe has been written by Eastern Europeans themselves that my interpretation should not be seen as involving a deliberate omission of facts but rather as emphasising those facts that, in the view of many Eastern Europeans, have been ignored for too long by Western European writers. As much as it is about the big picture of Eastern Europe, this book is therefore also about the missing details about the region.

I have tried to deal with some of the most common clichés and misperceptions of Eastern Europe to finally arrive at a point where, I hope, readers will understand why I am questioning the wisdom of continued reference to Eastern (or, indeed, Western) Europe. But I hope that I have avoided concentrating on what Eastern Europe *is not*, and have instead been able to show what *it is*. Of course, that is assuming that there is such a thing as Eastern Europe!

In 2004, the year of the accession of the eight new member states to the European Union, I was hoping in vain for a book to be written about Eastern Europe that would mark this truly remarkable event. At least in the English-speaking world, to my knowledge, no such book appeared on the history shelves of bookshops. Tourist guidebooks, seemingly unmoved and unimpressed by the big-bang enlargement, continued to feature Greece, which lies at the continent's easternmost edge, under the title of Western Europe and Slovenia, which lies west of Vienna, under the Eastern Europe section. So, I decided it was my turn to try to fill the gap. I hope that, on the twentieth anniversary of the fall of the Berlin Wall, my book will be only one of many to give much-needed attention to this continuing question of Western and Eastern Europe.

St Ferghal and the Globalisation of the Middle Ages

In 1994, in the small village of Vrhpolje in western Slovenia, only a dozen miles from the Italian border, there was a rather unusual public event, attended even by a high-ranking national politician. On a rock just outside the village, the villagers erected a monument, remembering a battle that took place exactly 1,600 years earlier between the Roman (Byzantine) Emperor Theodosius and the western usurper Eugenius. Although probably unknown to the reader, the battle was of considerable significance for the advancement of Christianity in the Roman Empire, since Theodosius was (at least formally) Christian and Eugenius was pagan, and the encounter is regarded as an important milestone in late Antiquity.[4]

The high profile of the celebration shows how even remote historical events are sometimes used by people in so-called Eastern Europe to claim the early participation of their lands (not even of their people in this case, as the Slavs would have not entered modern-day Slovenia until at least the sixth century!) in the development of Christendom and therefore, by implication, their stake in Europe. One may find such attempts rather desperate, especially if they involve a 1,600-year-old battle. But something else is also striking: how is it possible that villagers living in a place less than two hours drive away from Venice need so much to prove that they really belong to Europe? And what happened on the other side of the divide, in so-called Western Europe, to make territory only a few kilometres away seem so distant, so culturally different, that it deserves a special name – Eastern Europe?

---

[4] David Potter in *Roman Empire at Bay* gives the battle at Frigidus, as it is usually referred to, a significant parallel to that of the battle at Adrianopolis. However, it seems symptomatic that Potter places the battle in northern Italy, whereas it actually took place in what is today Slovenia. Could it be that one has some difficulty in placing an important historical event in Eastern Europe? (Routledge, 2004, pp. 529–533)

Although the example of, say, the Czech Republic and Germany is very similar, the situation is particularly shocking when one looks at Slovenia and Italy. Except in the years immediately after World War II, there was never really an Iron Curtain between Italy and Slovenia. In 2004, on EU Enlargement Day, Western media, hungry for iconic images of the Iron Curtain, repeatedly used photo-shots of the rather unthreatening fence between Italian Gorizia/Gorica and Slovenian Nova Gorica, a kind of mini-Berlin wall, but this was much to the amusement of the locals who were used to commuting daily through a nearby border post even in Communist times. (The purpose of that particular fence was more to mark the borderline than to prevent trespassing, and the most controversial event associated with it occurred in the 1950s, when a mob threw a high-ranking Slovenian clergyman over it into Italy, in an act masterminded by the Communist authorities.)

The truth was that, from the 1970s onwards, when Yugoslavia liberalised its border regime to allow for the development of its tourist industry and access to hard currency, Yugoslavs were free to travel anywhere they wished and as often as they wished. We were the privileged ones in the Communist world. Coming from a nearby town, I remember well how, in the years of my childhood, we used to go shopping in Italy almost every fortnight, bringing home items that were not available in Yugoslavia or were cheaper in Italy, like washing powder, fruits, coffee, etc.

I will return to the deeper significance of 'washing-powder tourism' later, but let me describe one more aspect of Cold War history at the border between Italy and Yugoslavia/Slovenia. Italians also came over to Slovenia in almost the same numbers to buy petrol and fresh meat or to indulge in Slovenian restaurants, casinos and good-value dental repairs. (In return, Yugoslav dinars, though not officially a convertible currency, were accepted in the shops of Trieste/Trst and Gorizia/Gorica.) Those Italian shoppers, gamblers and patients seemed almost completely ignorant about the country (Slovenia) they were

28

visiting and of the fact that it used to be a part of Italy and, before that, of the Venetian Republic. They seemed to know nothing of the centuries of shared history, as if Communist rule had simply erased them. In other words, during the Communist era it began to seem perfectly normal that Gorizia/Gorica or Trieste/Trst, with its Slovenian ethnic minority, should be labelled Western European, but that the immediate hinterland of Slovenia should be called an Eastern European land. And yet nobody was able to explain what exactly – other than Communism – made the Slovenian hinterland Eastern European and Trieste/Trst Western European.

In any account of European history, East and West first appear in connection with the eastern and western Roman Empire, i.e. the Byzantine Empire (called 'Roman' by Ottomans and Greeks and 'Greek' by the West) and the Latin Roman Empire (later referred to as the Frankish Empire). In 285 AD, the then Roman Emperor Diocletian moved the centre of the Empire to the East and divided it in two, drawing the dividing line across the province of Illyricum (now commonly known as the Western Balkans) roughly where Bosnia-Herzegovina is today. This delimitation, with slight changes, continued to mark political divisions – albeit by new and different polities – right up until the First World War. It also features prominently in Samuel Huntington's acclaimed work on the clash of civilisations[5].

Diocletian's aim was certainly not to create Eastern Europe – he did not think of East and West in those terms, nor, of course, did he think of Europe. He decided to divide the great empire to improve its management and above all its protection against various barbarians, mostly Germanic tribes and peoples – in other words (ironically) the future Europeans. Yet his choice of the division line was not purely arbitrary: he drew it where Latin influence faded and gave way to predominantly Greek influence. (The delimitation line was a couple of

---

[5] SP Huntington, *The Clash of Civilisations and the Remaking of the World Order,* The Free Press, 2002, pp. 157–161

hundred miles east of *Castra ad Fluvium Frigidus*, the Roman outpost near modern Vrhpolje, the Slovenian village mentioned above.) The division only concerned Mediterranean Europe; the vast areas north of it, where today lie other regions that are part of Eastern Europe, were not included in this mapping, as they were out of Roman military control. As we shall see, the Greek half would later play a very important role in the formation of Eastern Europe.

In the times with which we are concerned at this point, Europe as a political entity did not yet exist but the Roman and Greek worlds – as the spiritual foundations of Europe – did. In fact, with the demise of the Western Roman Empire, it was the Byzantine Empire which took over the role of 'Europe'. With Constantine, the capital of the Roman Empire was formally moved to the East. From then on, it was Byzantium, which regarded itself as the true Rome, as the 'world super-power', and, as such, it continued to intervene militarily not only in the Apennine Peninsula (one of the most splendid achievements of Byzantine art can be found in Ravenna, an Italian city just south of Venice) but even in the Iberian one. And the power of Byzantium began to gain additional momentum once the pagan West had been subdued by barbarians. The city, known also as Constantinople, was at the heart of a Christian Empire and it continued to flourish.

There have been ongoing attempts to define what made – or makes – Europe and its peoples European. The answer to this question proves not only to be far from obvious but also, and at the same time, highly divisive. In 2005, the draft European Constitution sparked some bitter exchanges on the issue of the role of Christianity in the formation of Europe. In the end – and this appeared to be done under the strong influence of French views on the relationship between Church and State – only a vague reference to 'religious inheritance' remained in the preamble of a document that was later to be abandoned anyway. Indeed, it seemed that the biggest problem for those who framed the EU Constitution was to name the sources that inspired the listed European values (rights of the individual, freedom, democracy, equality and the rule of law, justice and solidarity, diversity, pride in national identity and history, etc). The preamble specifically mentioned only 'cultural, religious and humanist inheritance', but failed to say which religion(s) were referred to. It did, however, mention Humanism as a particular philosophical view. But, some asked, if Humanism is there, why not mention Christianity too? The usual explanation at the time was that mentioning one religion would discriminate against the others. Moreover, the Crusades, the Inquisition, alleged Church tolerance of right-wing dictators and the like seemed to suggest that it would be politically incorrect to mention Christianity and its philosophical underpinning of Europe, even in such a benign text as the draft European Constitution.

Some Eastern Europeans, notably the Poles, were particularly unhappy about this omission of Christianity. The truth is that Humanism, which *was* mentioned, could only have taken root in an originally Christian environment. Moreover, it was mostly a Western and Central European phenomenon. In what I will later call 'Eastern Europe proper' (i.e. Orthodox Eastern Europe), Humanism only made an appearance from the late eighteenth century, and was even then seen as a Western importation. For an important part of Eastern Europe then, it was Christianity which provided the basic link with the rest of the Continent.[6]

Christianity was spread across the Roman Empire, both east and west, well before the arrival of the barbarians. In the east, the emperors were smart enough to abandon the ancient gods and to opt for the Christian God – be it out of genuine personal conversion or political

---

[6] 'In the prevailing narrative of European identity, "Europe" as an idea took shape only in the middle ages, when it succeeded the concept of Christendom. Both are Western: indeed, Christendom is often qualified as "western Christendom". In this narrative of Europe, Byzantium is conspicuously absent. In historiography about the expanding (western) Europe in the centuries after 1000, with its eastward adventures, Byzantium has usually featured as an ambivalence, less an ally than a duplicitous threat.' Quoted from Averil Cameron, *The Byzantines,* Blackwell, p. 165

convenience or both. They probably did so also because of the strong philosophical tradition they had inherited from classical Greece, which greatly influenced the first Church. The Western Roman Empire, on the other hand, did not recognise the expediency of Christianity and, arguably, this cost it its own existence.

Christianisation (or the creation of Christendom) was a cultural, political and also 'technological' and military process, a sort of globalisation of the early Middle Ages. The Western Roman Empire did not really care about it and disappeared; the Eastern Empire embraced it and survived much longer. The Roman (western) legacy was taken over by the Franks, who did recognise the political value of Christianity, while the Eastern Empire took over the legacy of the ancient Greeks. Thus, in the early Middle Ages, the Frankish Empire and the Byzantine Empire each stood at its own end of the European continent, fighting to subdue – in a political and religious sense – the peoples in-between, above all the Slavs, who entered Europe about that time and who were to become central to what would be known as Eastern Europe.

What was at stake for these early 'Eastern Europeans' in this process? Of major political importance in the region at that time were two peoples: the Bulgars, i.e. the early Bulgarians (actually of non-Slav origin) and Moravians (that is to say, the ancestors of the Czechs and the Slovaks), and both sought to manoeuvre between the two super-powers of the day, the Byzantine Empire and the Franks. Contrary to what geographical position might suggest, the Bulgars first sought Christian missionaries from the Franks, and the Moravians from the Byzantium. The Bulgars' approach to the Franks was not well received by the Byzantines and Constantinople reacted militarily. The final solution to what was, at first examination, a religious issue was reached at the ecumenical council in Constantinople where a majority of Eastern bishops decided that Bulgarians should fall under the religious rule of Constantinople rather than Rome. This left a profound mark on Bulgaria for the rest of its history: it acquired the Greek-influenced Cyrillic script and it remained in the realm of what later came to be known as Orthodox Christianity. The move also facilitated the Christianisation of Russians – the so-called Kiev Russians, i.e. the early ancestors of modern Russians and Ukrainians, who accepted Christianity in 987 AD.

In Moravia, the arrival of two Greek preachers, Cyril (also known as Constantine) and Methodius challenged the plans of Frankish missionaries and politicians. Under some pressure, the disciples of these two brothers were expelled and Moravia, together with Caranthania to the south (a principality of early Slovenians that covered roughly the same territory as the Austrian province of Carinthia today), came under Bavarian political influence. The Bavarians themselves had already been subdued by the Franks. (Both Bavarians and early Slovenians were converted about the same time and an excellent account of this in Latin has been preserved which is why we know so much about it.[7]) Christianisation was interrupted for a while by the arrival of the Avars (one of the ancestors of the Magyars) but Frankish help to the Slavs as they defended themselves against the new arrivals tightened the Bavarian/Frankish grip. After a brief but very important Irish mission (St Ferghal was bishop of Salzburg and he is still regarded as the Apostle of the Caranthanians, i.e. the early Slovenians), Caranthanians as well as other Slavs in Central Europe came under Germanic ecclesiastical control.

Further to the north, the early Bohemian rulers were looking westward too. Magdeburg became the centre for the Christianisation of western Slavs. In 964, Poles acquired Christianity from Bohemians through royal marriage. Later on, Poles and Czechs would be among the few Slavic nations able to establish their own church provinces directly

---

[7] Among those Slovenians that – like Karl Lavrenčič and Ljubo Sirc – settled in exile in the UK there was also a Catholic priest, Aloysius Kuhar. In 1949 he presented a doctoral dissertation at Cambridge under the title 'The conversion of the Slovenes and the German-Slav ethnic boundary in the eastern Alps'.

reporting to Rome, which would enable them to maintain, at least for some time, a fair degree of political independence.

The Hungarians, one of the non-Slavic nations of the Eastern Europe, initially came under Greek influence but German clergy prevailed after AD 980. Christianity was firmly established in the whole of Eastern Europe by the early years of the eleventh century. The exception was Lithuania, which only ceased to be formally pagan in 1385 when, again through marriage, its rulers accepted the Roman Catholic faith from Poles.

For the purpose of our further discussion it is important to note that Europe, in these early centuries, the Christendom of Charlemagne already included a great part of what today is popularly called Eastern Europe. By the fourteenth century, when 'Europe' got an even better-defined shape and the Holy Roman Empire of the German Nation (a union of small, principalities that were mostly but not exclusively German-speaking and that much later gave birth to what is today known as Germany) was firmly established, the political inclusion of the vast majority of modern Eastern Europe was even more evident.

Of course, there was no Western or Eastern Europe in the time of Charlemagne. To the Franks, the Slavs and Magyars were simply those (usually violent) invaders that needed to be dealt with in some way. Christianisation – even though in part carried out at sword-point – was a surprisingly civilised method of containing the Slavic (and later Magyar) menace, at least by the standards of the early Middle Ages. It was akin to the 'Stabilisation and Association Process' of the European Union in the Balkans today. To Christianise Slavs also meant turning them into allies, and allies – at least Christian allies – do not fight against each other. This stopped the advance of the Slav hordes but also made violence against them, now they were Christian, less acceptable morally. The new alliances also implied that, sooner or later, since they were at a lower level of political organisation, Slavs would be subdued by those who had already achieved a higher version of statehood, as the Franks had. It would, of course, be very premature to see in this any form of nationalism: the world of Charlemagne was not a world of ethnicities and even less so one of nations. It was a simple fact that, at a point when Christianity was gaining popularity, the Franks (as proto-Germans or proto-French or proto-Europeans) were at a stage of political organisation, which allowed the use (and misuse) of Christian religion for political purposes. For the Slavs to opt for Christianity may have meant an uncertain political future (although would there be any more certainty in confronting the Franks militarily?) but it also meant becoming a part of 'Europe'; a part of the globalisation of the Middle Ages.

One can only speculate about how much this globalisation was controversial at the time. How far the decision to accept Christianity was a conscious one is difficult to say, even for the Slavic rulers [8] On the other hand, some historians believe that it was not all about worldly interests, and that leaders such as Charlemagne were guided by genuine religious zeal[9].

The fact is that, culturally speaking, Christianisation gave the Slavs the first written texts in their own languages, facilitated access to the 'science' and arts of the day (at least to those very few at the time who could read and write) and generally brought them into the family of Christian nations, a sort of EU of the day. To expand the Kingdom of God in a faster and easier way, the missionaries made use of teaching and preaching in the vernacular, which also meant that these languages were given more defined written forms and were, ultimately, able to survive into the present day. The Freising Manuscripts, from the tenth and eleventh centuries, for example, which were written in early Slovenian, became the oldest written texts in any Slavic language in the Latin alphabet.

---

[8] Averil Cameron in *The Byzantines* writes that the Russian Vladimir's choice of Christianity was only made after '...research about merits of Islam, Roman Catholicism and the Orthodoxy represented by Byzantium'. Ibid., p. 173

[9] Derek Wilson, *Charlemagne, The Great Adventure* (Hutchinson, London 2005)

Twentieth-century historiography, as revised by the Communist authorities after the Second World War, tried to portray Christianisation primarily as the political subjugation of Slavs by Germans. (Some Slovenian politicians like to joke with their Irish counterparts about 'forgiving' them for St Fergal's conversion of the early Slovenians.) But while it is true that Slavs – with the possible exceptions of the Poles and the Czechs – lagged behind Western Europe in terms of political organisation and were politically subdued by the Germans, they did manage to survive as distinct ethnic groups until the present day. The fact that they were included in the family of Christian nations (with all the political consequences that followed this) certainly did help to prevent them being wiped out as pagans, which was the fate of some peoples of early medieval Europe who persisted in their pagan beliefs and practices.

By around the thirteenth century therefore, what today we call Eastern Europe was almost fully included in Christendom – the 'Europe' of the day. But there was one important distinction within the region: the peoples or ethnic groups of Eastern Europe, who received Christianity from Constantinople, adopted the Greek version of it, together with the Greek script (later developed into Cyrillic) and they accepted cultural and political influence from Byzantium. By contrast, Slovenians, Croats, Slovaks, Hungarians, Czechs and Poles received Christianity largely from the German church (and also, to a much lesser extent, from the Latin lands of modern northern Italy) and, consequently, they have adopted Latin script, Western thought and Western political organisation.

Eastern Europe was thus born out of the schism in the Church, the split that also occurred because of the political rivalry between the Byzantines and the Franks over the bodies and souls of the Slavs. However, this was not the same Eastern Europe that we know today; it was certainly not called 'Eastern Europe' then. At the head of medieval 'Eastern Europe' was Greece which was surrounded by

36

nations that had adopted the rites of Greek Christianity like the Serbs, the Bulgarians and the early Russians. Further west and north, however, there was another 'Eastern' Europe which used Western Christian rites. From this time to the present day, these two divisions of Eastern Europe have followed quite distinct paths. No wonder that, in the Middle Ages, no one thought of the Czechs or Slovenians as Eastern Europeans.

*

This debate about East, West and Christianity may sound rather academic but, deep down, it is central to the villagers of Vrhpolje, even if they might not formulate it in quite the same way. And not only to them; the late Pope John Paul II wrote in his last book: '...the division between the East and West was applied rather mechanically [during the Cold War without] taking account of the history of the peoples concerned... for the Poles it was unacceptable to be described as a people of the East'[10]. I will try to explain why both the villagers of Vrhpolje and the late Polish Pope have felt like this.

It is important to note, however, that the nations in the Middle Ages which chose the Eastern rite and Byzantine influence did not, in any way, make a foolish decision.[11] Quite the contrary: first, the choice was not a voluntary one but was a result of geographical proximity and/or *realpolitik*. Second, and more importantly, until about the eleventh century, Byzantium surpassed the Western European kingdoms and empires in almost every respect: culturally,

---

[10] *Memory and Identity,* Weidenfeld & Nicolson, London, 2005, p. 159

[11] It was much later that the term Byzantine was (wrongly) assigned a negative meaning. Averil Cameron in *The Byzantines* notes that the *Oxford English Reference Dictionary* explains the term with 'extremely complicated, inflexible or carried on by underhand means'. Ibid., p. 3. The same author also draws attention to the fact that even Byzantine studies, as an academic discipline, continue to be discriminated against: according to her, this area of research was not included in the five-year research programme on the transformation of the Roman world between AD 400 and AD 900 (see p. 5).

economically and militarily. In fact, one of the reasons why Diocletian moved the centre of gravity of the Empire to the East was that this part was much more civilised and prosperous[12]. People of Byzantium looked down on the then recently-converted barbarians in the west. For political leaders of 'Eastern Europe' in the Middle Ages, attachment to Byzantium rather than the West might well have looked more attractive for some very good reasons.

It is also interesting to note another factor: while the countries of today's Eastern Europe were certainly not at the core of Europe in the Middle Ages, they were by no means far from it. Economically speaking, historians talk about the axis of medieval Europe, drawn roughly from Antwerp (or later London) to Florence. For a very long time, this was the area of the most intense economic activity, enabled by fertile valleys, navigable rivers, access to the sea, dense population and large cities. Looking at the map, one can see that the Czech lands, Slovenia, Slovakia, Hungary and Poland did not really lie far from these centres of medieval Europe and were certainly not further from it than Spain, Portugal or Ireland. In fact, until about AD 1000, economic activity was pretty basic all over Europe. One economic historian has even calculated the GDP of Europe in those days as 400 dollars per capita[13], both in the East and the West. The European economy only really took off after the year 1000 and it is about that time that Western and Eastern Europe slowly began to diverge economically. For the year 1500, the same author has made the following estimates for GDP per capita (expressed in the same 1990 international dollars and for the territories of present-day countries): Austria 707, Finland 453, France 727, Germany 688, Italy 1,100, the Netherlands 761, Norway 640, Sweden 695, Switzerland 632, the UK 714, Ireland 526, Greece 433,

---

[12] For more details on the supremacy of Byzantium see Warren Treadgold, *A Concise History of Byzantium,* Palgrave, 2001

[13] Angus Maddison, *The World Economy: Historical Statistics* (OECD, 2003). The GDP per capita is estimated taking the 1990 world economy as the measure stick. Consequently, the calculated "currency" is called "1990 international Geary-Khamis dollars".

Portugal 606 and Spain 661. Unfortunately, the author presented only one, uniform figure for the entire Eastern Europe – 496 dollars. Although we can probably assume that, in the year 1500, the GDP of Central European countries was higher than in the Ottoman-occupied areas or in the sparsely populated areas of Eastern Europe 'proper', the gap between the East and West was beginning to show. On the other hand, we can also see that the economy was poor in other fringe countries as well, such as Ireland, Finland and Greece.

In addition, the Czechs, the Hungarians and the Poles (less so the 'unhistorical' nations such as the Slovenes) developed impressive enough political structures in the Middle Ages, comparable with what existed in the west. Above all, the medieval Bohemian (Czech) kings were among the key political players in Europe of the time. The reformation movement of the Czech Jan Hus preceded that of Luther, and the Czechs were at the centre of the all-European political dispute that caused the so-called Thirty Years' War, after which they were finally subdued by the Habsburgs. All in all, although political, social and economical development in parts of Eastern Europe in the Middle Ages began lagging behind that of mainstream Western Europe after the year 1000, there was little then to suggest a general backwardness of the region – and nothing that suggested a distinct name was required for this part of Europe.

The Slavs and the Rest of the Eastern Europeans

Things turned sour for Europe in the sixth century with the arrival of the Slavs, feared by both Germanic people and by the Byzantines. We do not know for sure whether violence against the old settlers (Germanic peoples, Greeks, Romans and other Romanised native peoples) was the dominant pattern when the Slavs moved in. There are also suggestions that, at least in some instances, they integrated into existing societies culturally, even when they prevailed ethnically. In any event they drew another wedge between the Franks and the Byzantines, obstructing the lines of communication between the two civilizations and the two superpowers of the day[14].

With their arrival, Slavs became the dominant element in Eastern Europe and they have been so ever since. In Western Europe the popular mind often equates Slavs with Russians and, since most of Eastern Europe (at least in recent history) was politically and militarily dominated by Slav Russia, concludes that other Eastern Europeans are Slavs too. However, there are a number of non-Slav peoples in Eastern Europe: none of the peoples of the Baltic nations are Slavs, nor are the Hungarians, the Romanians or the Albanians. The Greeks – the ultimate Eastern Europeans – are not Slavs. Eastern Europe is not exclusively Slav but is much more diverse.

Nor can the world east of the former Iron Curtain be simply reduced to a Russian influence zone, despite Russia's crucial role in the region in modern history. In fact, Russia only significantly entered the general history of Eastern Europe at quite a late date, not much before the reign of Peter the Great in the last decades of the seventeenth century. (Although Lithuanians and Poles, who had established a Commonwealth which was a key player in the region stretching from the Baltic to the Black Sea in the Middle Ages, were at loggerheads

---

[14] For a detailed study of the nature of the Slav (and others) migration see Peter Heather, *Empires and Barbarians,* McMillan, 2009, pp. 386–451

with their Eastern neighbours centuries earlier.) Peter the Great began building cultural ties with Western Europe at much the same time as he also began his territorial expansion to the West, with the Poles, the Baltic nations and the Finns being its first victims. From then on, Russia would continue to be seen as a threat to them.

After Christianisation, Poles and Czechs continued to enjoy relative political autonomy. This was not the case for Slovenians, who were soon submerged into Charlemagne's empire, or for Slovaks who came under Magyar rule. Further south-east, Serbs and Bulgarians too had their medieval states. For the south-eastern Slavs, the Greeks and some other nations in this part of Europe, however, the end of political autonomy came with the beginning of the Ottoman conquest of European territory in the fourteenth century. This also shook the Hungarian kingdom and the lands of the Moldavians and the Walachians, the ancestors of Romanians. The period of Ottoman rule and its key significance for this part of Eastern Europe will be looked at closely in Chapter 4. For now, it is important only to realise that the centuries of Ottoman rule (which, despite occasional uprisings, were largely peaceful times) somehow froze the history of south-eastern Europe until the nineteenth century when the Ottoman Empire began to collapse and Russia also started to exercise a stronger influence in the region.

The crumbling Ottoman Empire made possible the Russian advance towards the Black Sea and the Mediterranean. This went hand-in-hand with the rise of several, mostly (but not solely) Slavic and Orthodox Christian nations in parts of the falling Ottoman Empire. Thus the new Eastern question – who was to get the spoils from the final wars against the dying Ottoman Empire? – enabled Russia to gain a stronger influence in Eastern Europe. This was made easier by the common Slavonic and common religious (Orthodox Christian) roots of the Russians and the liberated Slavs. Shared Slavic origins appealed even to the Slavs of the West, like the Czechs and the Slovenians, who, at least at certain points in their history, saw in Russia a beacon of Slavic power and might and an inspiration against the rising German nationalism of the late nineteenth century. The so-called Pan-Slavic campaign, a nineteenth-century patriotic movement emphasising the unity of all Slavs, drew on the even older sources of the two preachers, the brothers Constantine and Methodius, mentioned in Chapter 1. Although the two were Greeks and not Slavs (just as St Patrick was not an ethnic Irishman), they continued to be known as the Apostles of the Slavs even in Catholic countries. The Pan-Slavic movement remained more or less on the level of an idea, with little practical consequences, but, even in the twentieth century, various Slovenian religious and patriotic societies bore the name of the two Greek brothers and today they are still associated with the Christian ecumenical movement.

In 2003, the Slovenian Government launched an initiative in the shape of the Forum of Slavic Cultures[15] as a framework for cultural exchange for all the Slavic nations. Not all of the Slavic countries embraced the idea with the same enthusiasm, which reflects not only the sometimes controversial nature of such associations within the Slavic world, but also the variety of historical experiences that individual Eastern European countries (and Slavic countries among them) have had with Russia. Some of them instinctively feared that the latter would dominate the Forum. Slovenia, on the other hand, is less troubled by such anxieties because there has never been a Russian military presence on Slovenian soil. (The only two exceptions are Russian prisoners of war held there during World War I and the brief presence of the Red Army in the north-eastern corner of Slovenia, formerly occupied by Hungary, immediately after World War II.) Nurturing this wholly non-controversial relationship was something that Slovenian politicians thought could only complement the country's main orientation towards the EU and NATO. This is not the case for some other Eastern European countries, whose relationships with Russia have been, at best, ambivalent both in the past and the present.

---

[15] http://www.fsk.si/index_en.php

One could speculate that, had it not been for the imposed Soviet domination of Central and Eastern Europe after World War II, the Russian language would spontaneously have become the *lingua franca* of the region. Indeed, I always feel strange resorting to English in order to speak to my Czech, Slovak or Polish friends. Speaking Russian, one of the great Slavic languages, would somehow be more natural. Some of the Czechs, Slovaks and Poles (at least those that went to school before 1990) may still be able to communicate in Russian but, even if they could speak it, they would usually refuse to do so because that language now seems to them the language of the former 'oppressor' – a sad fate for the native language of such great European spirits as Tolstoy, Dostoevsky, Solzhenitsyn and many others. For my part, as a former Yugoslav, I never *had* to learn Russian: following Tito's break with Stalin in 1948 (or, more correctly, Stalin's break with Tito) everything Russian had to disappear from politics, school classes and daily life, including the teaching of Russian. (My father was still learning Russian at school in the late 1940s but my mother, who was eight years younger, only studied English.)

As a result, most Eastern Europeans today prefer to use English. While Slavic languages have common roots, they are – again, contrary to popular perception – not close enough for us to be able to understand each other. Listening with great attention to somebody speaking Czech or Slovak or even Russian, I can pick up some individual words but Slovenian and, say, Czech are only related to one another in the same way that English and Dutch are. In other words, they may both be from the same family of languages, may both be 'close', but they are not close enough for easy interpretation. (Only Czechs and Slovaks, and Serbs and Croats can easily understand each other.) As a Slovenian, I am fluent in Croatian, which is probably the closest you can get to Slovenian, but even my knowledge of this language is more a product of the history of the last fifty years in Yugoslavia than of the language itself: the generation of Slovenians brought up and educated after 1990, and the collapse of Yugoslavia, find it much more difficult to understand Croatian. Croatians often say that they find it difficult to understand Slovenian anyway. In truth, Croatian and Slovenian are probably as close as Swedish, Norwegian and Danish – speakers of all three Nordic languages can just about understand one another.

The fact is that Eastern Europe is as diverse as Western Europe is. One does not normally describe, say, a Spaniard working in Ireland or England as a 'Western European'. This is because people appreciate and acknowledge that a Spaniard working as a teacher in the *Instituto Cervantes* in Dublin and an Italian student working in an Italian bar in London may have lots in common – they both speak languages from the same family and, in fact, their two languages are probably as close as Slovenian and Croatian – but they are still distinct. On the other hand, 'Eastern European' is often used as a shorthand term for a great number of nations and people and Eastern Europeans themselves find this somewhat demeaning. They feel reduced to membership of a kind of new tribe in this era of migrations.

The languages of this new tribe are also often a puzzle. A few years ago we had some Irish wine experts who came to visit Slovenia. They were truly impressed by what they saw and even more so by what they drank. One of them wrote a nice newspaper article, strongly praising the wines. However, he went on to say that Slovenian wine-makers should change the names on the bottle labels if they hoped to bring the wines over and sell them in the Irish market. According to him, the wine names were simply impenetrable.[16]

I was quite surprised to hear this comment coming from an Irishman – the Irish language is, if anything, further from English than Slovenian.

---

[16] 'What better way to express your distance from, or distaste for, a community or constituency – sexual or political – than to refuse to learn how to utter its name?... By mispronouncing a name, we mock or belittle its owner. By addressing a being or a body with the correct name, correctly delivered, we recognise and implicitly legitimise the person, group or institution,' writes Nigel Andrews ('Sound and fury', FT Magazine, April 15/16 2006)

I wondered whether, in the subtext of the wine experts comment, there was not perhaps some trace of the primordial, unconscious Slavophobia of non-Slavic Europe in the Middle Ages. Was this Slavophobia not also present when, in 2006, as Serbia was preparing for general elections which were once again interpreted as a choice between pro-European and nationalistic forces, a respected French scholar titled her essay 'The Contest between Serbia's European and Slavic Souls'?[17]

Or was the suggestion to change the names of the wines just a precaution against the resistance of potential buyers to the obscure and the unknown? Romanic nations (Spaniards, French, Italian, Portuguese) are associated with good food, easy living, sensuality and style; Germanic nations with technical superiority and enterprise. But, as the stereotypes of Eastern Europe demonstrate, Slavic nations are, at best, associated with folklore and, at worst, with shabbiness and misery. Those movies from Slavic Eastern Europe which win international prizes usually deal with issues like discrimination against the Roma community, ethnic conflicts, the trafficking of people and so on. These are undoubtedly valid and relevant themes but they are not a reflection of ordinary, everyday life in this part of Europe. The juries at international film festivals show less interest in general, human themes or even in the issues of social change that transition has brought to Eastern Europe and this has a self-censorship effect on Eastern European scriptwriters and directors who seem to have discovered that stereotypes are easier to sell. Similar stereotypes came into play when a controversial Irish politician was killed in a car crash in Moscow a few years ago. Some of the Irish papers readily assumed that the young Ukrainian woman, who was in the car with him, had been a prostitute. In fact, she had been an interpreter, working for a Czech legal firm.

It is probably for similar reasons that people seem to find political events in Eastern Europe just too difficult to comprehend and therefore

---

[17]See http://transatlantic.sais-jhu.edu/News_and_Commentary/Pond_serbia_jan07.pdf

too difficult to engage in. Again and again I read about the long history of violent conflicts in Eastern Europe, about a 'troubled' region, but I find it hard to think of any truly major conflict, before the wars in the former Yugoslavia, which involved the nations of Eastern Europe fighting amongst themselves. Certainly, history offers nothing on the scale of the conflicts between the French and the Germans, or the British and the French or the various civil wars which have plagued Western Europe. There were no Napoleons in Eastern Europe before Stalin, and the nations of Eastern Europe have lived in relative harmony with one another over the centuries. Probably the only major exception is the conflict between Poland and Russia. Of course, there was competition and occasional warfare between the Polish, Czech and Hungarian lords; Poles and Lithuanians fought Swedes over the Baltic territories; and Russians certainly fought over what today are Ukraine and Belarus. Then there were the Balkan wars which took place immediately before World War I. Savage? I am sure all these were, but so too was the Thirty Years' War. Further south, Slovenians and Croats are two neighbouring nations that have never waged war against one another. All in all, it is difficult to point at many bloody wars in Eastern Europe to match those of the West.

Before the twentieth century, wars in Eastern Europe were mostly fought with Russians, Ottomans and Hungarians; the latter came into the region after the Slavs and were soon seen as fearsome warriors. They populated a vast area, previously occupied by the Slavs, and were only finally halted by joint Slav and Frankish forces. If it had not been for the Hungarians, who ended up living between the lands of the Slovenians and the Slovaks, people in Western Europe today would be less likely to mix up the two nations. According to linguists, there are very important similarities between the Slovenian and the Slovak languages (although these similarities are not so strong that I don't have to resort to English when I speak to my Slovakian friends!). Looking on the map, one can see only a relatively short stretch of Austria (part of the country which contains a Croatian-speaking minority) lying between the extreme north-eastern corner of Slovenia and the extreme south-west of Slovakia, confirming the ancient connection. (In fact, after World War I, the peace conference in Paris briefly contemplated the idea of using this stretch of land as a corridor, politically linking what were then Czechoslovakia and Yugoslavia.[18])

Slav suspicions of Hungarians were reciprocated by the Hungarians. With Finns and Estonians as their closest and nearest ethnic relatives, Hungarians always felt like an isolated island in a Slavic sea, and they also felt threatened by Romanians and Austrians. Anxious to reach out from their isolation, they looked to the south, for access to the Adriatic Sea, and Croatia was indeed once included in their Kingdom. When Bosnia was annexed by Austria-Hungary, they tried in vain to have it included as well. And it was Hungary which, more than German-speaking Austria, most fiercely opposed the creation of a third, Slavic unit (in addition to the Austrian and Hungarian ones) in the Austro-Hungarian Empire, fearful of reducing their bargaining power versus the Austrians'.

With such an eloquent history, Hungary stands out among the nations of Eastern Europe as probably the one that had its own sovereign state for the longest time. Of course, this state took different forms and shapes over the centuries, and periods of sovereign rule were interrupted by shorter or longer periods of foreign domination, but overall Hungarians have the strongest tradition of statehood in the region. They are followed closely by the Poles. Croats and Serbs had powerful early medieval kingdoms which later disappeared. Serbs and Bulgarians only regained independence in the nineteenth century, as did the Greeks. Czechs finally lost their independence to Austrians in the seventeenth century. Most of Eastern Europe, as we shall see later, only fully regained its independence in the early twentieth century, as a result of the break-up of either the Ottoman Empire or Austria-Hungary.

---

[18] MacMillan, p. 246

There was, therefore, little possibility for armed conflicts between nations in Eastern Europe because, largely, such nation-states did not exist. What did exist was an empire – Austria-Hungary – and this was another reason for the absence of any major conflict among the peoples of Eastern Europe. When they were part of the Empire, there was little opportunity for wars between them. The only major conflict involving the nations of Eastern Europe was really the one with the Ottoman Empire. This was the second event after the Christian schism to alter the shape of Eastern Europe, and it created another, third tier in the region – the Balkans. The Byzantine Empire, the Orthodox part of Eastern Europe, played the key role in this conflict, and this is why I turn to it first.

The Byzantine Empire and Orthodox Eastern Europe 'Proper'

Marko Ivan Rupnik is a Catholic priest and a Jesuit from Slovenia. An artist and a philosopher, he runs a Jesuit centre for the study of Eastern spirituality and arts, called Centro Alleti[19] based in Rome. Together with the Czech Cardinal Špidlík, he is one of the leading figures behind the Catholic Church's efforts to reach out to the Orthodox world. This interest in things Orthodox intensified with the late Pope John Paul II, who was very impressed by Orthodox spirituality and, in particular, by the veneration of Mary in the Orthodox tradition. In 1996, he commissioned Father Rupnik to decorate the Papal chapel of *Redemptoris Mater* with the mosaics that became so typical of Rupnik and his team of artists: bright, vivid colours, unusual long faces and the choice of scenes all reminiscent of traditional Orthodox icon art. Indeed, Father Rupnik has dedicated himself to what could be called a reinvention of the Orthodox icon and its reintroduction into the sacred art of the West. Recently, his artistic vigour reached as far as the famous Fatima pilgrim site in Portugal (at another fringe of Europe) and to Lourdes in France. Under Benedict XIV, he is seen as part of a group of artists that the Pope wants to become the founders of a new Catholic art.

Father Rupnik comes from the picturesque Alpine village of Črni Vrh in central Slovenia, where even small peasant churches are covered in the typical artisan baroque decor, and the icon-like faces on his mosaics and paintings thus seem rather odd and even unnatural. In fact, the late Pope's interest in things Orthodox may be equally confusing for those trying to understand Eastern Europe. John Paul's homeland of Poland, like the rest of Central Europe, is traditionally Catholic, not Orthodox. His own comments from the balcony of St Peter's on the very day of his election that he had come from 'a far land' did not help

---

[19] See www.centroalleti.com

either. (His native city of Krakow is actually closer to Rome than Berlin.) His interest in Orthodox spirituality was, above all, religious, though some think that he was also concerned about mending the uneasy relationship that has existed between Russians and Poles through the centuries and thus, of course, between the Orthodox and the Catholic Church. Deep down, the interest of the late Slav Pope in things Orthodox was also a result of the fact that he was a Slav himself and that an important part of the Slav world is Orthodox.

In striving to be everything to everyone, Western Christianity (above all the Protestant churches, but also the Catholic Church) has gone to great lengths to strip itself of those elements that are conditioned by national cultures and old traditions, and which are not strictly related to religion as such. Churches started to use not only the vernacular but also plain everyday language. They absolved believers of the need for undue ceremonials, excessive piety and unnecessary regulations. Much, though not all, of the Church's 'red tape' has gone. Religion and its liturgies lie barer than ever before. This is certainly the case in the Catholic Church in English-speaking countries where the influence of the Anglican Church and the long disenfranchisement of the Catholic Church have made the interiors of the churches and the liturgy much simpler than they are in Central Europe where we appreciate more the appeal of the baroque.[20]

The faithful are not expected to engage in pious acts of faith anymore, in veneration of pictures and in other outer manifestations of their faith. But as a result of this 'depletion', some in the Catholic Church have begun to show greater interest in Orthodox Christianity and its spirituality, rich in ritual, lengthy ceremonies, incomprehensible ancient texts and holy pictures. Not surprisingly, there has been a

---

[20] An excellent account of this transformation of the Catholic Church in an English setting is contained in the hilarious *How Far Can you Go?* by David Lodge, Penguin Books 1981

revived interest in the Latin mass in the Catholic Church in recent times.[21]

The Catholic Church is a global, universal church that long insisted on operating in the 'trans-national' language of Latin only – the medieval equivalent to English today. On the other hand, the Orthodox Church approached the Slavs with a tailor-made scripture based on the Greek alphabet – Glagolitic, an older sister of the Cyrillic script, which appeared as early as the times of Constantine and Methodius. Unlike the Latin alphabet, Glagolitic (preserved into the twentieth century on the Croatian island of Krk and defended by a local bishop; a Slovene) had special characters for some of the sounds found in the early Slavic languages. For this reason, at least some of the corresponding sounds are today extinct in the Slavic languages that adopted the Latin script, which did not have such characters. The Glagolitic and later the Cyrillic script are (or were), therefore, better suited for writing down the Slavic languages. Indeed, in some ways, it could be said that Orthodox Christianity in general seems 'more Slavic', as it holds memories of the primordial unity of Slavs in the times of Constantine and Methodius. By the same token, the Slavs of Central Europe (Slovenians, Croats, Slovaks, Czechs, Poles) are somehow 'less Slav' than those further east, as their identity has also a strong imprint of the Germanic world – a subject I will deal with in Chapter 5.

Eastern Europe too is religiously and culturally divided between its own East and West (the products of Western and of Eastern Christian tradition), though it still has visible traces of the bond that once linked the two in a single Slavic entity. But, while the majority of Orthodox peoples are Slav, there are exceptions. The Romanians and the Greeks are two Orthodox nations that are not Slavic, and the Romanians have

---

[21] There is a danger, though, that the mystical and, to the majority of the faithful, incomprehensible Latin mass will cast a shadow on the efforts of the current pope Benedict XVI to emphasise rationality in the Catholic religion, as expressed in the Pope's address at Regensburg in September 2006, which sparked so much indignation amongst Muslims

a further distinction – not only do they write in a Latin script, they also speak a Latin language, the closest you can get to Italian anywhere in the world.

The word 'Orthodox' is often connected to the adjective 'Byzantine', though not entirely correctly. After the fall of the Western Roman Empire, the Eastern Empire used to be referred to simply as the Roman Empire, which reflected the fact that it regarded itself (rightfully so, as we saw in Chapter 1) as the real heir to Rome and as the (only) real defender of the Christian faith. It only began to be called 'Byzantium' after its fall in 1453; it got the name from a small town near Constantinople/Istanbul. (Interestingly, in some Slavic languages such as Slovenian, it is still called 'Carigrad', that is, the city of the Tsar or Emperor.)

While over the centuries Byzantium was more or less able to subdue or contain the military threat of the Bulgarians and the Slavs, their Muslim adversaries had gradually emerged as their most dangerous enemies. In addition, Byzantium was a theocratic state, its leaders taking theological issues very seriously – as seriously as perhaps only Charlemagne did in the West. Gradually this became a big problem in its relations with the West, where the papacy grew more and more independent and distant from Constantinople. Increasingly, the Holy Roman Empire on one hand and the Roman Empire of Constantinople on the other became irrelevant to each other in both a political and a religious sense. The preoccupation of Byzantium with the Slavs and later with the Arabs and the Ottomans, as well as the physical barriers (the wedge of Slavs between the two empires) exacerbated the problem. The theological differences were further complicated by disagreement over the Crusades. Ultimately, Byzantium was sacked by the Crusaders in 1204, which is still an issue for the Orthodox Church even today. There were attempts to restore the Empire and the union of the Church but, with only reluctant help offered by the West against Ottomans, often conditional on restoration of the Church unity,

Byzantium never really recovered. It was finally defeated by the Ottomans in 1453 and became Istanbul.

The later developments are the subject of the next chapter, which will show that it was during the Ottoman era that the term 'Eastern' finally began to take root, although in a rather different sense than the modern use of it would imply. At this stage it is important to recognise that, in the early Middle Ages up until the twelfth or even the thirteenth century, there was nothing 'Eastern' about the Byzantine Empire. Quite the contrary: the world then was Byzantium-centric. It was the Byzantine Empire which was in a position to declare who was at the centre and who was at the periphery of Europe, and it was Charlemagne and the popes who were trying hard to change this, first by the use of titles and language and then by *realpolitik*. It was only after about 1000 AD that Byzantium began slowly to decline, mainly because of its problems with the Arabs and later with the Ottomans. However, the association of Byzantium with bad government is mostly invention and not based on fact. There is nothing in its history to suggest that 'standards in public office' in Byzantium were any lower than those in contemporary Western Europe. It is, therefore, erroneous to cite the Byzantine origins of Eastern Europe as a contributing factor to the relative backwardness of the Eastern Europe in later centuries.

What was different was the relationship between the Church and the State. In the West, worldly rulers were busy thinking about how they could use the Church for their own political purposes. On the other hand, the Church, although it was eager to influence politics and even ran its own state, was busy fighting for its own independence. From today's perspective, it may seem that in the past the Church ruled the West, hand-in-hand with the secular powers. But this was only really true where and when it suited the latter and, despite many exceptions to the rule, the ideal of the separation of the clerical and the secular spheres of activity is intrinsic to Western Christianity. When the Church in the West interfered with politics, it tried to do so on its own terms. It did not allow secular rulers to deal with theological issues.

This was not the same in the Orthodox world where there was no attempt to conceal the unity of the two powers, sacred and secular. In fact, this unity was promoted and seen as a virtue, not primarily as an opportunity for political manipulation. Many rulers were genuinely concerned about theological issues and regarded themselves in the first instance as defenders of the faith. They also sincerely believed that the Christian God would punish them and destroy their earthly power if they did not uphold the true (Orthodox) Christian faith and lead their subjects to Him. Christianity was more important than the State. Of course, this is a generalisation and not all the Byzantine rulers were idealists. But, in the West, the Church, with its own State and an effective religious infrastructure, was, from early in its history, a power in its own right and, except during crises like the Crusades or the Reformation, it did not need defenders; it was secular rulers who needed the Church to provide validation of their rule. In other words, in the West, the Church was independent of the State, although the reverse was not necessarily the case; in the Byzantine world, it was not: the Church and the State were more or less the same and this was seen as a strength.[22]

This relationship between politics and religion in the Orthodox world led to the creation of national Churches and also to a degree of isolation from the rest of the world. It also enabled Orthodox nations to survive Ottoman rule by means of semi-autonomous structures within the Ottoman state when Byzantium (and other lands in the Balkans) were conquered by the Ottomans. But Ottoman rule also meant that these Orthodox Churches and their respective societies were protected from (or deprived of) the Reformation and the Enlightenment. They were 'protected' from what in the draft European Constitution was the only explicitly cited philosophical underpinning of Europe, with all the consequences for economic, societal and political developments that

---

[22] See for example Bertrand Russell: 'In the Eastern Church, the patriarch of Constantinople never acquired either that independence of secular authority or that superiority to other ecclesiastics that was achieved by the Pope.' (*The History of Western Philosophy*, Simon & Schuster, p. 390)

that entailed. It is in this isolation that the roots of the relative backwardness of the Balkans should be sought.[23]

What about the relationship of Byzantium with the rest of Eastern Europe? Byzantine influence was limited to the south-east and the far east of Europe – it never managed to establish itself in the areas of modern Hungary, Poland or the Czech Republic, i.e. Central Europe. The centre of the Byzantine world was originally, of course, Greece, and it is the Orthodox tradition that connects that country with other Eastern European countries, at least with those that share the tradition. (It is the experience of long rule by the Ottomans which, in another sense, connects it to the Balkans where Greece is even today an influential state.) At first, even Russia was only indirectly influenced by the Byzantine tradition via Bulgaria but, after the fall of Byzantium and with the decline of Bulgaria under the Ottomans, it was this country which took over the role of the centre of the Orthodox world. Moscow became the 'third Rome' and, with its rising military strength, Russia became the ultimate regional power even in areas where Byzantium never managed to establish itself – in Eastern Europe proper. It was thus Russia which, by a twist of history and with the help of Orthodox Christianity, gradually became synonymous with Eastern Europe. This happened despite the fact that, for centuries, Russian influence did not reach further west beyond the Ukraine and Poland and that, before World War II and its aftermath, Russians never ventured into Central Europe.

---

[23] Averil Cameron writes that it was with the Ottoman conquest of south-eastern Europe, that the region was closed off from the intellectual developments that had existed within Byzantine society and led to the 'permanent identification of Byzantium with absolutism on the one hand and Orthodox spirituality on the other. The negativity that surrounds the idea of Byzantium is especially evident in the modern discourse of "balkanism", and the idea of "byzantinism", or "byzantinismus" plays an important part among the negative characteristics that mark out the Balkans from "Europe" and "the West".' See Cameron, pp.175–76. For more on the image of the Balkans see Maria Todorova's seminal work *Imagining the Balkans*

Culturally, 'Eastern Europe proper' was deeply influenced by the Orthodox legacy of the Byzantine Empire. In addition, this part of Eastern Europe was also shielded from the effects of the Enlightenment. This had political and social consequences such as the late abolition of serfdom in the region. Also, the Orthodox tradition was primarily concerned with the heavenly and holy and much less with the affairs of this world. All this led to a growing gap in economic and social development between Central Europe and Eastern Europe proper. Natural conditions made things even worse: east of Central Europe, there lay large swathes of sparsely inhabited lands. In Western Europe, at the height of the Middle Ages, farming became very intensive (to keep up with the increasing demands of the densely populated areas of Western Europe) but there was little need for such intensification in 'Eastern Europe proper'. In fact, even the gap between Western Europe and Central Europe is often explained by the fact that the West was increasingly turning to more sophisticated forms of agriculture (dairy and meat), as well as to non-agricultural economic activities. In these circumstances, Central Europe became the granary of Western Europe. Because of its proximity to Western Europe, it could still successfully manage to export and transport agricultural products to the West which – until the arrival of the railway – was not possible or viable for countries lying further to the East. To get going, 'Eastern Europe proper' lacked both an economic stimulant that was physically near enough and a philosophic ambition within its own culture. In the absence of both, it began drifting away from Central Europe, and also, of course, from its cultural roots in the south-east where the Ottomans now ruled.

I have already mentioned the growing economic gap between Eastern and Western Europe from the year 1000 and, in particular, from 1500 onwards. Sadly, we have no data (or, rather, the better word is estimates) for individual Eastern European countries for that period. For the year 1600, the average GDP in Eastern Europe is estimated at 548 dollars, while that of Austria was already 837 dollars. The Netherlands had nearly doubled its national income since 1500 to

1,381 dollars, the highest in Europe, while that of the UK was 974. Greece and Finland remained below the Eastern Europe average but Spain and Portugal took off, largely because of the discoveries in the New World[24]. A hundred years later, in 1700, the Eastern European average GDP per capita is estimated at 606 dollars. That of the UK is then almost double that figure (1,250) and the Netherlands has got an even firmer lead with 2,130 dollars. Greece and Finland, each at its own fringe of Europe, were again lagging behind or were just about catching up with the Eastern European average.

Over the centuries, things turned upside down in Eastern Europe. In the early Middle Ages, Greek Byzantium stood a good chance of becoming the master even in Central Europe. Greek missionaries, most notably Cyril and Methodius, operated among the early Czechs, Slovaks and Slovenians but were ultimately evicted and replaced by German (and for a short period Irish) missionaries. Thus these lands were already lost to Byzantium and Orthodox Christianity at a very early stage of history. The schism in the Church created the gap between Central and Eastern Europe. The gap between Central Europe and the Balkans, however, was created and then cemented by the Ottoman conquest. Greece, once the pivot of Europe and later of Eastern Europe and Orthodox Christianity, lost its primacy of the East and even of Orthodox Christianity. Such was the extent of this loss that today we are not accustomed to think of Greece as an Eastern European (and Balkan) country at all. In another twist of history, after its accession to the EU, Greece began to feature in the popular mind as a Western European country. In a way, the job of those medieval barbarians from the West had been completed.

---

[24] All data is from Maddison

Islam Creates the Balkans

With the Ottoman conquest of Byzantium (Constantinople) in 1453, the lands that once marked the dividing line between the Western and Eastern Roman empires and later between the Franks and the Greeks were turned into a buffer-zone between the Ottoman Empire and the Holy Roman Empire. Although at one point the Ottomans made it as far as Vienna, they never permanently settled west of this East-West divide. The fall of Constantinople as the capital of an already fading Eastern Empire seemed to make it easy for the Ottomans to conquer the rest of that Empire. But Western Europe finally pulled itself together to establish a more coordinated and effective defence against the Ottomans and did not allow them to progress further west.

Europe, as shaped by the Ottoman invasion, then remained almost the same until the nineteenth century. The establishment of 'Turkey in Europe', as the Ottoman-occupied zones were known and, on the other side of the divide, the rise of the Habsburg Empire in Central Europe, effectively separated Eastern Europe into three tiers:

- the Balkans (south-east Europe) which was occupied by the Turks and consisted of modern-day Greece, Bulgaria, Serbia, Montenegro, Bosnia, Albania, Macedonia, parts of Romania and parts of what was then Hungary
- Central Europe and the Baltic shores (i.e. Eastern Europeans within the Habsburg or German Empire) which consisted of the modern-day Czech Republic, Poland, Slovakia, Slovenia, the core of Hungary, the shores of the Baltic states, parts of modern day Romania and most of Croatia
- Eastern Europe 'proper' (i.e. the part of Eastern Europe that remained under the more or less strong influence of Russia) which was made up of modern-day Belarus, Ukraine, parts of Poland, Romania and parts of the Baltic states.

As we can see, there was (and still is today) a degree of overlap. Parts of Poland and the Baltic states, though generally Catholic or Protestant, also experienced some influence from Russian Orthodoxy. Further south, the Balkans shared both the Orthodox Christian tradition and the experience of the Ottoman occupation but the Ottomans also occupied parts of Catholic Hungary, Croatia and Bosnia. (The reason why Medjugorje, the world-famous pilgrim site in the ethnic-Croatian part of Bosnia, called Herzegovina, is managed by the Franciscan order is that they were the only Catholic clergy allowed to operate by the Ottomans.) As a result, the Balkans is where the Western (Catholic), Eastern-Orthodox and Oriental-Muslim traditions meet. They form the true multicultural region of Europe and they were like that long before modern Turks, Moroccans, Algerians and other Muslims set foot in Western Europe.

Another important thing to note about the Balkans is that, while the concept of 'Eastern Europe' today includes Central Europe and 'Eastern Europe proper', the war in former Yugoslavia has resulted in the Balkans somehow being excluded from it. The rise of Serbian nationalism under Milošević (with some help from the Croatian nationalism of Franjo Tudjman, although the two cannot be compared exactly) resulted in the somewhat surprising fact that Yugoslavia, once the most progressive part of the former Communist world, began to lag seriously behind the rest of the Communist world in terms of democratic development. Not only Milošević but also the Serbian Academy of Science and the overwhelming majority of the Serbian public entirely missed the point about what was happening in the late 1980s. While rightly concerned that Yugoslavia was going to fall apart and fearing that this would eventually result in ethnic communities of Serbs scattered across Yugoslavia and no longer living in one single state (something that the Serbs had achieved with the creation of the Yugoslav Kingdom at the end of World War I), they decided to prevent that by the use of the (federal) army over which they had control. It was a tragic mistake for everyone in Yugoslavia but – strategically speaking – it was worst of all for the Serbs. (What would have happened had the Serbs, instead of opting for violent nationalism, put themselves at the front of an all-Yugoslav, genuinely democratic movement which favoured federalism, thus preserving Yugoslavia?) They paid a high price and, until after the fall of Milošević, they were excluded from the European Union's plans for the Balkans, being overtaken by Bosnia-Herzegovina, Macedonia and even rebel Montenegro.

Only after arms were finally laid down with the NATO intervention in Serbia and Kosovo in 1999, and United Nations administration was imposed in Kosovo the very same year, were efforts begun on the side of the Balkan nations and Brussels to allow them gradually back into the political realm of Eastern Europe by putting them on the EU track through what is still called the Stabilisation and Association process[25]
a mixture of foreign, security and enlargement policy, tailor-made for the Western Balkans.

But let's return to the fifteenth century! While the Balkans were being conquered by the Ottomans, the Central European part of Eastern Europe, through its early adoption of Western Christianity and through its contact with the Germanic world, managed to maintain its inclusion in the Western world. It enjoyed relative political stability and the vicinity of the economic axis of Europe. Nations further east were at a lower socio-economic stage of development (for reasons explained

---

[25] Croats and Serbs find it difficult to comprehend that Bulgaria and Romania, for example, are already EU members, but they are not (yet). From the point of view of the general level of development, the feelings of the Croats and the Serbs are entirely justified. In 1990, before the war started in former Yugoslavia, the GDP of what was then Serbia/Montenegro was USD 5,249 and that of Croatia USD 7,351. In the same year, the GDP of Bulgaria was USD 5,597 and that of Romania USD 3,511. Figures are from Maddison, p. 101 and 105. To this purely economic comparison one should add the fact that both Serbia and above all Croatia were much more open to the West than the other two countries, at least in terms of the flow of ideas and the ability to travel freely to the West. With the entrance of Romania into the EU in 2006, the Serbs were required to have visas to enter a country whose citizens once only dreamt of travel to Serbia.

earlier) and nations under Ottoman rule lost contact with mainstream Europe.

The Ottoman era in Europe is also the time when the term 'Eastern Europe' was coined. According to Wolff[26], the modern concept of Eastern Europe originates in the attempts of eighteenth-century philosophers to find a physical location for the state of mind they considered opposite to that of the Enlightenment. Although they believed so deeply in the importance of reasoning and empirical evidence, the key figures in this process, Voltaire and Rousseau, seem never actually to have visited Eastern Europe. Further handicapped by the embryonic state of the geographical and linguistic sciences of the time, their accounts suggested a place of uniform and unvarying poverty, backwardness, ruthlessness and dullness – a vision that has in large measure persisted until the present. It was only the rise of a number of independent states in Central and Eastern Europe after World War I that, as we will see in Chapter 6, began to change this picture. Unfortunately, Yalta and the Iron Curtain cemented this view for another fifty years.

Western writers during the period of Ottoman rule in south-east Europe found a particular satisfaction in their discovery of these lands, either in reality (by means of travel) or in imagination. 'Eastern Europe' in those times could mean the Ottoman-occupied lands of south-east Europe or what I have called 'Eastern Europe proper'. There was not a clear definition, nor was there a need for one. The Oriental elements of the Ottoman Empire inspired as much fear as fascination, and both feelings informed views of the countries beyond the 'Iron Curtain' of the time. Facts about these countries did not really matter so much as the imagination. The alleged ferocity of the bloodthirsty Ottomans, which began to be associated with the lands beyond the Curtain, somehow impressed the Western world. The Dracula character stems from this source. It has been recently revisited by

---

[26] See *Inventing Eastern Europe* in the Key literature section.

Elizabeth Kostova in her novel *The Historian*[27], where Eastern Europe is once again confusedly associated with vampires, ferocity and backwardness, and the ill-informed text is littered with historic inaccuracies. A similar contemporary stereotype was created by Hollywood in the film *Hostel* in which two naïve American students, seeking sex and drugs, end up in a torture chamber in Slovakia. The movie deeply annoyed my Slovakian friends, who were astonished by the numerous factual errors about Slovakia in the script. Stereotypes can be reinforced by movies from Eastern Europe itself. One evening in May 2009 in the 'Film Huis' in the Hague, after the screening of a Bosnian movie about the dilemmas of a group of desperate and lonely women in a remote village, a Bosnian lady said to me: 'This is the picture the people of Western Europe want to have about us: poor and nice. It is a strange sort of comfort for a Dutchman leaving the cinema and thinking, "Thank God I am not Bosnian! We may be in the midst of a global financial crisis but I will be looked after; my comfortable life as a European citizen will not be disrupted that greatly. I will not be left to my own destiny and to the elements somewhere up in the Bosnian hills with no future to look forward to."'

After the fall of the Berlin Wall, the Western world is once again fascinated by the East. The West, with its ambivalent relationship to its own consumerism, looks at the East with a mixture of disdain, naïvety and envy. In the alleged poverty of the East, it hopes to find confirmation of its own high standards of living and, in the idealised primordial warmth of the East, it looks for social conditions it has long lost. All these simplifications, stereotypes and inaccuracies are, of course, very human but they have practical social, political and even economic consequences for Eastern Europe. They do not exactly attract tourists, they do not make Eastern Europe (or for that matter the

---

[27] (Little, Brown 2005). E.g. Kostova writes about 'Ottoman elements' in 1930s Ljubljana, the Slovenian capital's architecture (a detail flatly wrong) or about 'one little Austrian church' in the same city (the church in Ljubljana could have looked Austrian only because Slovenia was for ages part of the same cultural environment, not because there would be anything Austrian on the church itself.)

Balkans) seem an ideal business location and, as we saw with the Dutch salesman of the Slovenian brand, they do not boost sales of products from Eastern Europe. (Perhaps they will draw more people to the cinema to watch Bosnian movies!)

Ottoman rule and the state of war that existed between the Ottoman Empire and the West also meant that, for a very long period, the nations subdued by the Ottomans were cut off from developments in other parts of Europe. As has already been noted, Humanism and the Enlightenment, which Europe today considers as its philosophical pillars (remember the preamble of the European Constitution), by-passed these countries. Once the subject nations emerged out of the ashes of the Ottoman Empire in the early twentieth century, it was not only the Churches of East and West (Orthodox on one side and Catholic or Protestant on the other) which were separated but also their respective societies. However, it was not, as it is sometimes argued, primarily because of the (alleged) backwardness of the Ottoman Empire that Balkan countries went into a decline. (If the Ottomans had been that backward, they would certainly not have managed to gain such an empire in Europe!) The backwardness into which the Balkans slid under Ottoman rule had more to do with the carelessness of the Ottoman rulers towards the subject nations and, of course, with the lack of contact with the rest of Europe.

Defining what exactly the Balkans are remains problematic. The European Commission now regards the Western Balkans (the simple term 'Balkans' is apparently too discredited) as the following countries: Albania, Bosnia & Herzegovina, Kosovo, Macedonia, Montenegro and Serbia. Romania, Bulgaria (the home of the actual Balkan mountains) Croatia and even Greece were excluded. Apparently, the Balkans is not a geographic or historic term, but a political one, a state of mind, and inclusion or exclusion from this concept depends on political circumstances, such as membership or even expected membership of the European Union. Naturally, such a view does not encourage anyone to stay in the Balkans long. Only the

Serbian Government website seems to be brave enough to describe their country as a Balkan one.[28]

Much to the annoyance of Slovenians, my country too is sometimes lumped together under the heading of the Balkans, for the sole reason that it became a part of Yugoslavia after World War I. At least until Slovenia's entry into the European Union, attempts by Slovenians to disassociate the country from the (alleged) negative attributes of the Balkans have usually been met by derision.

There is a similar issue in the Baltic states. One morning not so long ago, in a live Irish radio programme from the Estonian capital, when most listeners seemed to be busy phoning in to find out how much a pint costs there, an Irish lady living in Tallinn was talking about the difference between Estonia and the two other Baltic countries. She said that the food in Tallinn restaurants had a different, Nordic influence. Estonians themselves would have an easy explanation for that. For them Estonian food does not just have a Nordic influence; it *is* Nordic. This is because Estonians are not entirely happy with the idea of being only Baltic. They consider themselves Nordic, like the Swedes or the Finns. It is Western Europeans who feel they can, for the sake of simplification, call Estonians Baltic and not Nordic, simply because it is somehow assumed that a former Communist country cannot be placed in the same group as 'fancy' countries like Sweden.

Turning back to the Balkans, the name actually comes from a mountain chain in southern Bulgaria, on the border with Greece. (This is why the Bulgarian national airline used to be called Balkan Airlines before it closed down in 2002.) To the Bulgarians, their Balkan heights are what the Alps are to the Swiss and other Alpine nations, and they are none too happy to see other nations in the region being described as Balkan. The fact that the Balkan Mountains actually lie in Bulgaria probably led diplomats to re-brand the region as the Western Balkans,

---

[28] See http://www.srbija.sr.gov.yu/pages/article.php?id=30

although geographically this makes little sense. Where is the Eastern Balkans? In Bulgaria, Romania and Greece, some would reply. But then what exactly makes the Western Balkans so different from the Eastern Balkans? Is it just the difference between the former Yugoslavia and Albania on one hand, and Bulgaria, Romania and Greece on the other? But then what exactly connects these last three countries? With some justification – given that it was the Ottoman Empire that created the Balkans politically – one could call Turkey part of the Eastern Balkans too. But where does the peninsula end and the mainland begin in the case of the Balkans? For some, the Balkans begins in Trieste/Trst, for others it is already present in Munich or at Vienna *Südbahnhof* railway station – anywhere where people from the Balkans can be seen.

Historically, the Balkans means the area of south-east Europe that used to be under Ottoman rule. (It was once also a way of naming Europe, as seen from Ottoman Istanbul and, before that, from Byzantine Constantinople.) The loss of the Balkans was a terrible blow to the Turks and, in some quarters of Turkey, it is a matter for grief and regret even today. The Turkish perspective is, naturally, quite different from that of the Greeks and the Slavic nations of south-east Europe. For the Turks, these nations stabbed the Ottoman Empire in the back, after it had provided for centuries a stability and a peace that the region had not previously enjoyed, and this is a view that is not entirely without substance.

Some Turks concluded that the key mistake that led to the loss of the Balkans was made with the decision not to force the Muslim religion upon the subject people[29], which would also confirm the view that the Orthodox Church needs to be credited for the survival of the Balkan nations. In Bosnia, on the other hand, the lack of a comparably strong Church organisation and the presence of a distinctive Christian sect

---

[29] See Tanil Bora, *Turkish national identity, Turkish nationalism and the Balkan problem* in *the Balkans, A Mirror of the New International Order,* Günay Göksu Özdoğan and Kemâli Saybaşih (eds.), Marmara Univeristy, 1995.

called Bogomilism, with some theological features close to Islam, made conversion easier. Essentially, though, accepting Islam under Ottoman rule meant, above all, an opportunity to climb up the social ladder of Bosnia at the time. Still, only a relatively small part of the Balkans actually converted to Islam and these peoples were seen by their Orthodox neighbours simply as 'Turks' until very recently. (This is where the historical roots for the dislike between the Serbs and the Albanians in Kosovo or the Serbs and the Muslims in Bosnia lie.) Today, Islamic Eastern Europe includes Albania, Kosovo, parts of Macedonia and Bosnia – places that are usually associated with ethnic conflicts and/or war. But very few people in the West realise that these are actually the only European countries with an indigenous Muslim population. It is *the* centre of European Islam, much more so than the UK, France or Germany where Muslim populations are the product of much more recent immigration from non-European countries. In addition, Bosnia, long before the war started, had a historic record of genuine religious tolerance and a tradition of secular Islam. In fact, secular Bosnian Islam was actually the main building element in the country that today we call Bosnia & Herzegovina – a fact that the local ethnic Serbs and Croats do not much like to hear. While some may have doubts whether Turkey lies in Europe, there is certainly no doubt about the position of Bosnia. Even in Kosovo, where today co-habitation between ethnic Serbs and ethnic Albanians is a rare occurrence, in the past ethnic Albanians were the main guardians of the Orthodox monasteries.

In 1987, I did a month of military service (in the Yugoslav Army) in Sarajevo and only returned for a visit there again in 2000 as a civil servant of the independent Slovenia to watch Slovenian experts undertaking the dangerous work of de-mining the numerous mine-fields across the country. The city was still impressive, definitely European, albeit with a touch of Orient. For some time, the country has been trying very hard (but perhaps not hard enough) to reach an agreement between the Serbs, the Bosniaks and the Croats over future constitutional arrangements. The EU even went so far as to bend slightly what were originally very tough criteria, which led the country to sign the Stabilisation and Association Agreement in June 2008 – something that was met with great joy all over Bosnia-Herzegovina. But the momentum seems somehow lost at the time of writing and the EU and the US are very concerned again that the ethnically almost purified Republika Srpska will simply go its own way, uninterested in doing business with the much less effective Federation, i.e. the Muslim-Croat part of the country. But imagine what a more sensible approach by the Serbs and Muslims alike could do for the country, making it, at some point in the future, the first EU member state with a sizeable indigenous Muslim population – a move that could change the way some people look at the prospect of Turkish EU membership too. In a period of tense relations between the Western (Christian) world and the Muslim world, this could be an added value for the European Union.

Further south-east, Albania, which is a majority Muslim country, is making an enormous effort to shake off the legacy of its brutal Communist past. It has a long way to go, although, by entering NATO in 2009, it made a great leap forward. Its neighbour and cousin, Kosovo, the sanctuary of Orthodox Serbia, finally got its long-awaited independence in 2008. No one saw it as an ideal solution. But in the end most governments in the West realised that an undefined status for Kosovo presented a greater risk for itself and the region than an independent Kosovo did for the stability of Serbia. (In a strange way it was a compliment to Serbia that it could handle this truly difficult loss – a loss that could have probably been prevented even after the fall of Milošević, had the assassination of Prime Minister Djindjić in 2003 not set the clocks back.) On the other hand, it is true that Serbia did not really want Kosovo, at least not in its entirety – it only wanted the territory, together with its Serbs and the Serbian heritage, but not its ethnic Albanians. Even discounting the efforts by Serbia to make Kosovo's independence as bitter and meaningless as possible, the two ethnic communities will still have to learn how to live together and give up the tribal culture that pervades almost all spheres of life. Blood feuds and forced marriages for both women and men are the most serious issues not only for Kosovo itself but also for other European countries such as Switzerland, where Kosovo Albanians live in considerable numbers. If Kosovo manages to overcome its problems, it may, in the near future, forge ahead of Albania. The fact is that Kosovo, because its people have lived in autonomy in the relatively well-off Yugoslavia, even today has the strongest potential of all the Albanian-populated areas in the region.

Kosovo is not the only nation to have fled Serbia. Even the Serbians' Montenegrin half-brothers, led by their shrewd Prime Minister Djukanović, went their own way in 2006, fed up with the eternal internal struggle in Serbia between liberal pro-Europeanism and the various incarnations of post-Milošević nationalism. After the victory of the liberal Boris Tadić at both presidential and parliamentary elections in 2008, the EU generously opened its gate for Serbia through the signing of the Stabilisation and Association Agreement. However, the coalition in Belgrade could not govern without the input of the party of Milošević, much changed and repentant of its past though it is. The radical opposition seems weaker than ever at the time of writing but the decision to aim for EU membership is not unanimously and unconditionally approved by the majority of Serbs: the opposition leader Tomislav Nikolić has publicly declared that Serbia should become a member of the EU (though not at any cost) but that it should also have a special relationship with Russia. And in addition, there is always the temptation to continue to grieve over the loss of Kosovo and to win elections on that basis.

Another neighbour of Kosovo, Macedonia, is perhaps the most vulnerable part of the Balkans at the moment. The wounds of the relatively short inter-ethnic conflict between Albanians and Macedonians in 2001 have been largely healed but the country is still troubled by intra-ethnic conflict within the Albanian community (with strong connections to organised crime), by the party political struggle between the shrewd, very young but also very popular conservatives and the more sophisticated left, and by the ongoing saga of the dispute with Greece over the use of the name 'Macedonia'. Greece feels that its poor and weak western neighbour has stolen the name, traditionally belonging to Greece, and wants it changed. The Macedonians are proving stubborn and will not give it up, even if EU and NATO membership are at stake. (Greece effectively blocked the entry of Macedonia into NATO at the organisation's summit in Bucharest in April of 2008.) Indeed, they are not being helpful at all: to make a point they named the country's main airport after Alexander the Great and furbished the Prime Minister's office in Skopje with locally excavated artefacts from Greek times rather than with artefacts of early Slavic Christianity in the area, which would be more characteristically Macedonian. Some Macedonians have gone as far as claiming that they are descendants of the ancient Macedonians, a claim which makes the Greeks furious. Now, it is very likely that some of the DNA of ancient Macedonians (ethnically different from but culturally very similar to the Hellenic-Greeks) is in the veins of the contemporary Macedonians, but they share most of it with the Slavs who arrived in these parts almost a thousand years later. And it is here that one should look for the real causes of the bickering: northern parts of Greece are still populated by the remnants of a Slavic (Macedonian) population and their modest claims for a kind of minority status seem to threaten the sense of national unity that Greece has developed since World War I. In addition, this same population stood firmly on the Communist side in the Greek civil war in the late 1940s. Today, there seems to be a lack of sensitivity on both sides – in Greece, where fears of this weak neighbour are grossly exaggerated and the risk that Macedonia, if it is held back from EU and NATO membership, would turn into a liability for the region, is underestimated, as it is in Macedonia, where compromise is not seen as a virtue and history is used to create myths that are of little help to the economic and social conditions of people.

*

In the late nineteenth century, the Ottoman Empire began to collapse and a number of south-eastern European countries partly restored their autonomy, inspired by humanistic and Enlightenment ideals which had taken so much longer to arrive in the region[30]. Through the two so-called Balkan wars on the eve of World War I, Greece, Serbia, Bulgaria and Rumania fully regained their independence. After World War I, the new Kingdom of Yugoslavia, in reality an extension of the restored Serbian monarchy, took over most of the Balkan Peninsula. The victors of the war denied Austria-Hungary its ambitions to extend further south-east, but allowed Serbia to extend its influence further north-west. The Germanic drive towards the Adriatic was halted, but not everyone was happy or too hopeful about the prospects of the new Yugoslav state either. I will look at this period of restoration and relative prosperity in the Balkans and the wider Eastern Europe in Chapter 6. Before that I wish to look more closely at why Germany and Austria, once the two key players in Eastern Europe and the main actors in two world wars, lost this position of influence, and how that affected Eastern Europe.

---

[30] It is interesting to note how the Enlightenment ideals clashed with the Byzantine legacy – at least that was how the Greeks of the day saw this legacy. Averil Cameron writes in *The Byzantines*: 'Against the Enlightenment ideas with which the idea of Greek independence had been invested Byzantium seemed to belong to a tradition of darkness and medievaldom, and to be dangerously associated, especially through the Church, with Ottoman rule...' (p. 177).

The Germans and Central Europe

A few years ago, attending a Christmas display in an Irish town, I almost felt at home looking at the large nativity scene that had been set up. It was like those we have in Slovenia: a manger with the Holy Family, hills, covered with layers of moss, and scores of plastic shepherds, sheep, cattle and other little figures. Looking at the label beneath it, I discovered that the crib was actually from Slovenia. This was a typical Eastern European custom, the label said.

In fact, the nativity scene originated in Italy, but it spread across Europe and took root in Central Europe in particular, especially in the Alpine countries. It is not only an Eastern European custom. In the Christmas period, nativity scenes can be seen in Italy, Austria, Bavaria and Switzerland as much as in Slovenia.

The Irish 'Eastern European' nativity scene was undoubtedly the result of sincere efforts by the local people to pay attention to the traditions of a new member state of the EU. Yet it was also an example of the popular mindset that tends to associate the unknown and the traditional with Eastern Europe, something which – as we saw earlier – novelists and moviemakers also do. In this instance, however, the perceived 'backwardness' is seen in what seems a more positive light. It is seen as a demonstration of appreciation for past traditions, and the absence of hi-tech consumerism. Indeed, Eastern Europe is sometimes seen or portrayed as a living folk museum, where antique objects, customs and old-fashioned people can be observed, but also where traditions provide the only aesthetic luxuries in an otherwise grim life. In this way, the East is perceived and imagined as the opposite of the wealthy, modern and technologically advanced West.

Often Communism also saw the traditional as a sign of backwardness and, as a reaction, the post-Communist era in Eastern Europe has seen a revival of respect for the old customs. At the same time, after the changes, the traditional was equally often seen as incompatible with modernity and consumerism. The result is that Eastern Europeans generally have very mixed attitudes towards their heritage. The majority of them are certainly proud of their past and their traditions. However, they do not wish to live in an ethnographic museum in which they themselves are the objects of undue attention. They do not wish others to see their respect for tradition as a sign of backwardness – if, indeed, this respect is any stronger in Eastern European countries than it is in countries like Italy, Switzerland, Germany or other places where old folk customs are on the tourist menu. They do not wish to be seen as a living laboratory of the European past, where those from the West can observe how they themselves used to look ages ago. They reject the kind of attitude that the first Europeans in the New World showed towards the natives there. And they certainly reject the vision of the folk traditions of Eastern Europe as something exotic, alien to European culture, almost non-European.

Such an unwanted picture of Eastern Europe is at the centre of *Molvania*[31] – a book (and associated website) that appeared a few years ago in which odd Eastern European customs feature prominently. (Some bookstores put it among the travel books and some among the humour.) It is brilliantly designed to look like a standard guidebook with details about history, national parks, beaches, where to go, where to stay and where to eat. The only problem is that it is about an invented, stereotypical Eastern European country named Molvania – an Eastern European version of Borat's Kazakhstan. Of course, the shabbiness, ugliness, dullness, backwardness and poverty of the place is emphasised to the point of absurdity but the book is perhaps not so absurd that some people will not start searching for Molvania on the map! *Molvania* was not the first book of its kind, though. In the more sophisticated *Why Come to Slaka?* by Malcom Bradbury, first published in the 1980s, Slaka was the name of another invented Eastern European country that was held up to ridicule.

---

[31] www.molvania.com

Of course, these books should be accepted with a good sense of humour – even by Eastern Europeans themselves. Books on stereotypes about individual Western European nations have been published too[32]. In the case of Eastern Europe, though, there is an evident lack of knowledge of stereotypes of *individual* Eastern European nations. Writers just make fun of Eastern Europeans as a single entity. There seems to be nobody to be able to make a specific joke about, say, the Slovenians, or to know stereotypes about the Moldavians. Also, a lot of this general negative stereotyping is about what remains of the Communist era. These reminders of the past are undoubtedly still around in many places in Eastern Europe and they deserve to be laughed at – or, perhaps, they should attract concern that they still exist and continue to have a negative influence on people's lives.

But let's go back to that Christmas nativity scene. This custom is one of the elements that connects Eastern Europe with the Germanic world. All around Central Europe, several other signs of popular piety, such as small roadside chapels and wooden crucifixions in the countryside, are signs of a common Catholic tradition that unites the region[33]. Almost equally powerful in their own way, popular foods like strudel, dumplings, sausages and sauerkraut cross the boundaries of the former Habsburg lands. With some simplification it could be said that Greece, Orthodox Christianity and Russia created 'Eastern Europe proper', and Orthodox Christianity and Ottoman rule were crucial for the formation of south-east Europe or the Balkans. In Central Europe, though, it was the Germanic influence that was the most important.

The Germanic encounter with Eastern Europeans began as early as the times of the Franks, and it continued throughout the centuries of the Holy Roman Empire of the German Nation and the Austrian Habsburg

---

[32] See e.g. Richard Hill, *We Europeans,* Europublications 1997.
[33] Fichtner, p. 145.

Empire right up to the Nazi period. It was German speakers who pushed the Slavs towards the east and the south, colonising the more sparsely populated areas and bringing with them also urban culture and advanced agricultural techniques. This colonisation was organised but it did not yet have the characteristics of planned Germanisation. Whether the peasants were Slav or German did not make much difference to the feudal lords, most of whom (though not all) were German-speaking. Still, the net effect was that the Germanic-Slavic ethnic border was pushed further to the east and to the south. So, for example, in Carinthia, the southern province of Austria, which in the early Middle Ages was the political centre of the early Slovenians, there is now only a minority Slovenian community. Gradually, this silent change of the ethnic structure began to have political implications, as Germanic nobility took lands away from indigenous landlords, usually of local ethnic origin. In the nineteenth century, in the era of revolutions and the births of nation states, this became a serious issue. The relatively peaceful coexistence of Slavs and Germans began to collapse, destroying the Central European idyll. Slavic nations within the Austrian Empire began to fight for their place under the sun. Usually the battle took the peaceful form of vigorous political and civil campaigns for the public use of the local Slavic language and enforcement of already existing legislation in favour of equality. There was pressure to change the signage on public offices, pubs and shops. There were colourful political confrontations on urban and provincial councils, and there was competition between rival societies and social clubs, sport organisations, etc. However, clashes between protesters and police occurred and there were even casualties. The fight was mostly fought in the cities, because it was there that most German speakers resided. Sometimes they even formed a majority of the urban population, surrounded by an almost exclusively Slavic countryside.

The term 'Central Europe' (sometimes the German name *Mitteleuropa* is used) came into existence during the process of German nation-building. It was a Prussian invention, which was then taken over by the

Habsburgs and later also by the Visegrad countries (Poland, the Czech Republic, Slovakia and Hungary) and has been used right up to the present day. Nineteenth-century debates about German identity and the future of the nation, focused around the issue of securing the resources needed for the economic development of the German empire. While colonies were considered as an option, many Germans thought that Germany should, above all, build a wider sphere of influence for itself, both economic and political, in its immediate neighbourhood. Although these ideas were also used by extreme nationalists and ultimately degenerated into an excuse for the Nazi conquest of Europe, their origins were more benign. One of the best-known advocates of the creation of a Central Europe as a single economic and political area was Friedrich Naumann, a liberal member of the German parliament. Naumann's book with the same title (*The Central Europe*[34]) advocated the creation of a loose, above all economic, European federation to include Germany, Austria-Hungary, Poland and countries further afield, from the Vistula river to the Vosges Mountains and from Galicia to Lake Constance, a 'welding together of the German Empire and the Austro-Hungarian Dual Monarchy'. The entity would use German as its main official language (a suggestion that did not sound presumptuous at the time) but all the nations would be equal and would have the right to use their own vernaculars. Reading the book, one finds surprising similarities not only to the Euro-jargon of the present EU but also to issues discussed today in relation to the European Constitution. For example, Naumann writes that issues of 'creed and nationalities' 'should not be subjected to any centralised regulation... nor will the super-State have anything to do with school affairs'. Similarly, the 'much disputed language question must be left to the decision of the individual States', as should internal administration. He talks about some of the legislation being dealt with by a 'Mid-European Commission' and housed in one place, with specialised offices in Frankfurt, Hamburg, Berlin, Vienna and Prague. (Yes, Eastern Europe is not excluded from his plans, and yet the

---

[34] Published by Alfred A. Knopf, New York, 1917.

European Union as we know it today still finds it so difficult to agree to have the seat of at least one common agency situated within one of the member states that have recently joined it.) The 'super-State' would be governed by a 'treaty system as the basis of Mid-European unity' and so on.

Naumann's idea was buried in the ashes of two world wars (although a similar idea of an All-Danube federation resurfaced in the 1930s and 1940s among Eastern European intellectuals). It was, however, resurrected as an all-European idea in the project of the European Communities and later the European Union, which is essentially a German and French idea. However, two world wars were needed before Europe looked at this idea seriously.

The First World War offered a number of Eastern European countries the opportunity to escape Germanic influence and regain independence. Poland was resurrected, and two new, rather artificial states were created: Czechoslovakia and Yugoslavia. Yet, during World War I, many Slovenians, Czechs, Slovaks and Poles fought as Austrian soldiers – a duty they must have performed with very mixed feelings. Austria was increasingly a bad mother to them, favouring its German-speaking children. But the prospect of, say, Russian rule for Polish people or Italian rule for Slovenia was not particular inspiring either[35]. From that point of view, the creation of independent national or multinational Slavic states, however imperfect, was seen as probably the best possible outcome. In the end, World War I left Germany and Austria humiliated, reduced, and perhaps, as German-speaking subjects themselves felt, misunderstood. Austrians in particular felt that they had been betrayed by the Slavs, and they did not recover for some time. The feeling of loss is not completely gone even today. In a private discussion about Kosovo in 2007, a high-ranking Austrian diplomat remarked to an embittered Serbian minister

---

[35] In Trieste/Trst region, the ambitions for Italian national unity found the local ethnic Slovenians on the Austrian side of the fence.

that Austria too had had to go through the process of losing part of its territory.

But it is World War II which has had an even more dramatic and decisive impact on the living memory of the peoples of Eastern Europe. In that war, Slavs were second only to Jews in the list of those for whom the Nazis had a murderous contempt[36]. They were also second only to Jews in the numbers who fell victim to the Nazis. (In Yugoslavia, Albania and Greece, the troops of Fascist Italy also committed horrible crimes against civilian populations – a fact later obscured when the Italians switched allegiance in 1943.) This altered relationships in Eastern Europe dramatically, reducing the appeal of German culture and its role there virtually to nothing. After World War I, Austria had to renounce its rule over large swathes of Eastern Europe and also its own idea of a Central Europe. After World War II, Germany had to withdraw from Eastern Europe behind new and well-defined borders, which were cemented by the new post-war international order. This means that, after more than a thousand years of shared history, the Slavic and the Germanic worlds were finally separated. The Iron Curtain only reinforced this.

However, it was not only that German troops had to withdraw from the land they occupied. Local ethnic German populations in the Czech lands, in Poland, Slovenia and elsewhere were often forced (or simply chose) to leave. Certainly the majority of these local ethnic Germans (although not all of them) had often been sympathetic to Hitler and the Nazis and some were certainly involved in war crimes too. Under special decrees by the then Czech President Beneš, almost all Czech Germans were forced to leave the country, leading to a bitterness that

---

[36] 'The Nazis treated Western Europeans with some respect, if only the better to exploit them, and Western Europeans returned the compliment by doing relatively little to disrupt or oppose the German war effort. In eastern and south-eastern Europe the occupying Germans were merciless, and not only because local partisans – in Greece, Yugoslavia and Ukraine especially – fought a relentless if hopeless battle against them.' See Tony Judt, *Postwar: A History of Europe since 1945*, William Heinemann, London, 2005, p. 17.

is still around today. It was only partially alleviated by a solemn declaration made by Vaclav Havel and Helmut Kohl in 1992, addressing both the 1938 Munich Agreement which led to the annexation by Hitler of the areas of the Czech lands populated by ethnic Germans and the forced expulsion of ethnic Germans from the same areas after World War II[37].

In Slovenia, there was not exactly a forced expulsion but the measures adopted against the 'sympathisers of the occupying forces' had a similar effect on a much smaller scale. Here, the situation was even more complicated. While most ethnic Germans were living in the urban centres of Yugoslavia before World War II, there was also the very special case of an ethnic-German community in south-east Slovenia, around the town of Kočevje. These so-called Kočevje (or Gottscheer) Germans were the remains of medieval German colonisation, a closely-knit community that preserved an archaic form of German, with some influence from Slovenian. They had worked hard in past centuries, clearing the woods to create a flourishing farming society which lived in a fairly harmonious relationship with the surrounding ethnic Slovenians. But, when World War II broke out, the Kočevje area fell into the Italian zone of occupation. So Hitler and Mussolini agreed to have them removed from their traditional homes and sent to places from which local Slovenians had been expelled and despatched to Germany, Serbia and elsewhere.

Once the Kočevje Germans had left, their villages were largely destroyed by the Italian army to prevent them from being used by the resistance movement that had headquarters in the woods in the area. What remained of the houses and churches of Kočevje Germans after the Italians had left was then finally destroyed by the Communist authorities after the war, clearing the area of any memory of the

---

[37] For a detailed account of Czech-German relations in the nineteenth and twentieth centuries see Z. Benes et al, *Facing History – The evolution of Czech-German relations in the Czech provinces, 1848–1948,* 2002 (published in English in the Czech Republic).

community including, above all, its religious monuments. Moreover, as we shall see later, this battered-down area also became the killing fields for Slovenian and other Yugoslav anti-Communist troops after the war. After all this, it was turned into an off-limits area, where only hunting havens and nuclear-proof shelters for the Slovenian political elite were allowed to exist. The Kočevje Germans were not mentioned again until after 1990 (and nor were the massacres of anti-Communists). Only then was it possible to state that Slovenia was poorer without a community that by that time had been long scattered around the globe. It was too late: another precious link between Eastern Europe and ethnic Germans had been destroyed. Now the local museum dedicated to their memory and the books published about them are unable to return the people to the overgrown villages, lost amidst the dense forests that surround them.

People in Eastern Europe who can still see some merits in the old Austrian Empire, despite all its faults, are today at great risk of being seen as naïve and nostalgic. The unspeakable suffering caused to Slav nations by the Nazis (including many Austrians) erased most of the good memories of the times of earlier Hapsburg rule. Any claim today that a more restrained German nationalism and a decision to make Austria-Hungary a federal state with strong autonomy for the Slavic nations would have saved it and perhaps would have created a European model-state, is easily dismissed as pure speculation. The world of Central Europe as it existed for several centuries was finally lost in the ashes of World War II. Even the German language, which was the *lingua franca* of Central Europe for centuries, was replaced by English, a language that belongs to modern times and to the wider world but not to the region. Not only that: the general public both in German-speaking and Slavic countries has today almost completely lost its awareness of a shared history and of being a part of the same Central European culture. History, as taught under Communism, assisted greatly in this process: not only did we learn to dislike Germans because of what the Nazis did to our countries during World War II but also because they used to be our feudal lords.

This loss is particularly striking in the case of Czechs and Slovenians, who were most closely connected with Germany and/or Austria. (The latter, through both its name and its geographical position, could actually be claimed as an Eastern European country: Österreich means 'Eastern Kingdom' and, if you are travelling from Prague or Ljubljana, you have to head *east* if you want to get to Vienna.) Popular wisdom in Vienna has it that, among the oldest Viennese families, there are those whose family names still sound Slavic even though they are written in a German form. And it would be difficult for Slovenians to find a nation that was closer to them, in its political history or even ethnogenesis, than Austria. (Because of centuries in which they had a common border with Hungarian-ruled Croats, Slovenians have had less political and even cultural interaction with their immediate Slavic neighbours who are otherwise closest to them in language.) Or as an American writer put it: 'The bulk of Slovenians… had become "Austrian" (though not German) in the twelfth and fourteenth centuries. Culturally, but not linguistically, they are Austrians and with a certain amount of exaggeration one might say that the central and east Austrians are the only Germanised Slovenes, and the Slovenes the only non-Germanised Austrians – a definition that both sides would find most displeasing.'[38] Not necessarily so. Long before the above words were written, Ivan Cankar, the greatest Slovenian writer and most outspoken socialist politician of his time, who vigorously advocated the political union of Slovenians and other neighbouring Slavs, said in a public speech in 1913: 'In the cultural, let alone the linguistic sense there does not exist a Yugoslav question! Perhaps it did exist once, but it was resolved when the south Slav tribe split into four nations with four fully independent cultural lives. We are brothers in blood, cousins at least as far as the language is concerned; but in culture, as a result of several centuries of separate education, we are more alien to each other than is our Gorenjska Region farmer distant to a Tyrolian one or a winemaker from Gorica to one from Furlany.'

---

[38] Von Kuehnelt Leddihn, p. 261.

In the 1990s, Poland, the Czech Republic, Slovakia and Hungary, the countries known as the Višegrad Four (after the town of Višegrad in Hungary where, in 1335, the kings of Bohemia, Hungary and Poland met), reclaimed the title of Central Europe. Intellectuals in these countries helped to reinstate the concept as they had already attempted to do during the Communist era. The political grouping of the Višegrad Four was meant to facilitate the path of these countries towards accession into the EU but the philosophical underpinning of the idea (the restoration of Central Europe) met with a very mixed reaction in Western Europe. In some instances, it was interpreted as an unnecessary attempt to change the reality of the East-West division or as a handy excuse to avoid the label 'Eastern' or even as laying claim to a (Western) European legacy that was not to be shared with Eastern Europeans. Apparently, the idea of Central Europe challenged deeply ingrained views of Eastern Europe as a region inherently different and distant from the West, perhaps even as a place that needs to exist in order to justify the existence of 'Western Europe'. (Interestingly, doubts may have been expressed about the existence of a Central European identity but there never seem to be any doubts that an Eastern European identity exists.)

For Slovenia which, for much of its history, was the one nation in Eastern Europe (apart from the Czech Republic) which was most closely linked to Austria, laying claim to Central European status was an even more difficult task. (Mostly because of the imagined baggage it brought from its years as part of Yugoslavia, Slovenia also failed to earn membership in the Višegrad group which it desperately wanted at the time in order to speed up its approach to the EU and NATO and, above all, to decouple itself from the Balkans. In the end, Slovenia joined the EU at the same time as the Višegrad Four but they got NATO membership a few years earlier.) At the end of Word War I, Slovenians, together with Croats and Serbs living within Austria-Hungary, proclaimed the State of the Slovenians, Croats and Serbs. This included modern-day Slovenia, Croatia, Bosnia-Herzegovina and the northern Serbian province of Vojvodina with its sizeable Hungarian population and other ethnic minorities. However, nobody wanted to recognise this state and the Italians, following a secret clause in the London Treaty that rewarded Italy for its change of sides, invaded most of what today is western Slovenia, including the village of Vrhpolje mentioned in Chapter 1. In these circumstances, the young State of the Slovenians, Croats and Serbs was pressed to merge with the Kingdom of Serbia under the Serbian crown – something that Slovenians, let alone Croats, never really wanted. (Despite their pan-Slavic feelings for the Serbs, both Slovenes and Croats had been appalled by the assassination of the Austrian archduke in Sarajevo in 1914 by a Serbian nationalist.) Suddenly, the Slovenians found themselves in the same state with lands and peoples that for centuries had been part of the former Ottoman Empire, and with which they only shared either distant Slavic roots or sometimes not even those.

To understand the later conflicts within Yugoslavia, it is therefore important to note that Yugoslavia was not a natural choice for many of the peoples included in it – except for the Serbs, who saw it as an extension of their own kingdom. True, the Yugoslav (meaning 'south Slav') kingdom did provide for a temporary shelter from German nationalism[39]. At the same time, Slovenia was dragged into a Balkan context where it had never belonged. Since Serbia had undoubtedly been a Balkan country, the newly-created Yugoslavia (for all practical purposes an extension of Serbia) came to also be called a Balkan country. Slovenia, as part of Yugoslavia, was suddenly a part of the Balkans as well. Slovenians deeply sympathised with the Serbian

---

[39] In Carinthia, the southern-Austrian province, where a large Slovenian minority remained after the borders between the Yugoslav kingdom and Austria were finally defined, the successors of the late Mr Haider as the county's former Governor continue to vigorously oppose the erection of bi-lingual topographic signs as required by Austrian Constitutional Court and in accordance with Austrian international obligations, but this – surprisingly – receives little attention in the European media, perhaps because such attitudes are difficult to reconcile with the otherwise positive image of Austria. Chauvinists are usually sought elsewhere – in Eastern Europe.

struggle for independence from the Ottomans but, as Ivan Cankar pointed out in the speech already quoted, they did not feel culturally close enough to make them feel like citizens of the same country. There was little common history and memory to share, except pan-Slavic myths. Not surprisingly, therefore, the concept of the Yugoslav nation never really took off.

The point here is not, as some might wrongly assume, to suggest that Slovenians are 'any better' than any of the Balkan nations. After all, Serbs have, in many ways, had a much more glorious and certainly more dramatic history than Slovenians have had. So too, one could argue, have the Croats. The point is to reject the lumping of small nations into geopolitically convenient units – even when neither history or geography nor cultural proximity allow for such manipulation. This is not pettiness on the part of Eastern European nations but a demonstration of their wish to be respected and identified in the way they see themselves.

Rebellion, Emancipation and Totalitarianisms

In Ottoman-ruled south-east Europe, the nineteenth century was marked by uprisings against the Turkish overlords. Greeks started rebelling in 1821 and finally succeeded in gaining their independence a few years later. The liberation movement started in Bulgaria at about the same time. Nationhood was won in the late 1870s in at least part of the country but full independence was achieved only at the beginning of the twentieth century. The timeframe was similar for Serbia. The principalities of Walachia and Moldavia were united under the name of Romania in the mid-nineteenth century. A modernisation of Romanian society, previously under Ottoman and Russian rule, commenced and full independence from the Ottomans was achieved in 1877. Indeed, this was a landmark year for all the countries of south-east Europe because of Russia's victory over the Ottoman Empire which helped them in their own fight for independence.

In Central Europe too, as we saw earlier, the nineteenth century was a time of nationalism, echoing the general mood in the rest of Europe. Germany and Italy were created at much the same time – both are relatively young nation-states too! While in south-east Europe the national movements were directed against the Ottomans, in Central Europe the main 'adversaries' were the Germans and the Austrians. A revolutionary spirit spread among the Slavic nations within the Austria-Hungary Empire (and Prussia) and, as has already been mentioned in the previous chapter, a cultural struggle began. This struggle was strongly reflected in the arts of Eastern European countries of the time. As SA Mansbach has written, 'As a consequence of the nineteenth- and twentieth-century limitations on the free exercise of political, economic, and personal liberties in the regions of the Continent subject to Romanov, Hohenzollern, Habsburg, and Ottoman control, the visual arts assumed a primary responsibility as cultural custodian for the respective "subject nations". Hence, artists of these regions often elected to emphasise national individuality rather than universality. They responded variously to a public demand for expressions of national self-consciousness through which an emerging nation might stake its claim simultaneously to singularity and to membership in a modern world. Such profession of national identity through the medium of progressive art was a cultural phenomenon as widespread in Eastern Europe as it was rare in the west. Among the developed political states of Western Europe, modern national identity has been (and remains) the province of politicians and statesmen and only incidentally the concern of the artists; but then the nations of the West have often been free to express their identities politically.'[40]

Mansbach certainly has a point, although art *was* used for nationalist/political purposes in many of the Western countries too. His text appears in a catalogue published on the occasion of an exhibition of the masterpieces of visual art from the ten new member states organised during the Irish Presidency of the European Union in 2004. While this was a most commendable (and costly!) exercise on the part of the Irish Government, it also nevertheless confirmed that the eight new entrants that came from Central and Eastern Europe were very diverse nations, even if they did share some traits in common, of which the national movement of the nineteenth century is certainly one. This was also recognised by Mansbach himself, who later in the text adds: 'Despite a shared pre-First World War history of foreign domination, the nations represented in this exhibition nevertheless reveal strikingly disparate cultural traditions, social structures, and political formations.'

Towards the end of the nineteenth century, the nationalist movements culminated in demands that the Slavic nations should at least have autonomy within the Empire. However, there was no general consensus as to how this was to be achieved; before the end of the First World War, few Slavs thought of fully independent states. Most hoped that a federal solution within the Empire could be reached, others that the help of the Allies, including Russia, should be sought. Amongst

---

[40] SA Mansbach in *New Frontiers – art from new EU member states,* National Gallery of Ireland, 2004.

German and Austrian politicians, a minority were sympathetic to the ideas of federalism but most were carried along on the tide of ethnic German nationalism. Austria feared losing access to the Adriatic, and losing Bosnia to Serbia. Above all, Austrians were scared of an outright end to the Empire, something that eventually happened perhaps precisely because of the way the crisis was handled before it developed into the First World War.

The war made little sense to the nations of Eastern Europe. It was not their war, although, as it dragged on, they realised that it might represent an opportunity for their national aspirations. Some of the Eastern European nations were in quite a complex situation. While the Austrian-occupied part of Poland became the centre of the movement to restore the Polish state, part of the country was also under the rule of Russia, one of the Allies in the war. Some in the Polish national movement thought that they could somehow, perhaps by playing the Slavic card, achieve (limited) independence with the help of Russia. At the same time, many Western Allies thought that Russia should not be upset by the idea of a Polish state but that the Poles should be left in the Russian zone of influence. Things became more complicated for the Poles with the Communist revolution in Russia when Lenin went on to sign a separate truce with the Central Powers. But these complications did not only apply to the Poles: the Western Allies were also concerned that a social revolution might spread from Russia, which is why an independent Polish state came to be seen as a welcome buffer zone[41]. In the Czech and the Slovak lands there was also a pro-Western and a pro-Russian strand within the national movement.

In the very last months of the war, Eastern European nations one by one proclaimed their independence from the Austro-Hungarian Empire (and from Prussia). They were encouraged by American involvement in the war and, above all, by President Wilson's Fourteen Points, the

---

[41] Wandycz, pp. 180–200

most important of which acknowledged the right of national self-determination. Although there were (and are) conflicting interpretations of what exactly President Wilson meant by this, it marked the beginning of the love-affair of Eastern Europe with the USA at a time when the 'old' Europe was not able to sort out its own problems[42].

Sometimes only indirectly, Russia played an important and positive role in the independence struggle of a large number of Eastern European nations. (Although the Slovenians and the Croats, for example, were not really affected by Russia.) For a time it appeared that perhaps even the long-standing conflict with the Poles could be resolved. All this was suddenly brought to a halt by the Soviet revolution and soon a rather sinister Russian policy towards Eastern Europe emerged. One can only wonder how Russia and Eastern Europe would look today if there had been no Communist revolution – most likely Russia would have been held in much higher esteem by many of the Eastern European nations.

Elsewhere, the new Austrian republic built on the ruins of the Austrian Empire, humiliated and frustrated, shrank to little more than the German-speaking part of the former Empire. The Slavic nationalisms of the nineteenth century created an image of the Empire that, perhaps, it did not deserve, and it was this image that the triumphant new

---

[42] The right of nations for self-determination again re-surfaced at the time of the break-up of Yugoslavia – another occasion when the Continent was unable to solve its own affairs and US involvement was needed – and most recently with the issue of Kosovo. Do the people of Kosovo possess this right? An answer to this question is expected in 2010 from the International Court of Justice in The Hague but what will it be? Most believe that it is not possible to give a straightforward answer because there seems to be no legal definition of what exactly constitutes a 'people' and the principle of self-determination is in conflict today with another and more recent principle of inviolability of territorial integrity of states. Interestingly enough, as many as 36 countries from across the globe sent their submissions to that question to the ICJ in the Spring of 2009.

Eastern European nations were happy to abandon and venture enthusiastically into an unknown future on their own.

A look at the map of post-World War I Eastern Europe reveals a hugely reduced Hungary, an enlarged Romania, and an independent Albania, Bulgaria and Greece. On the shores of the Baltic Sea, Lithuania, Latvia and Estonia won independence from Tsarist Russia. After many years, Poland finally regained its independence. Two new states appear on the map as well: Czechoslovakia and Yugoslavia.

Yugoslavia and Czechoslovakia were a novelty, a product of Wilson's previously unheard-of principle of the self-determination of nations. They were an artificial attempt to create a nation by forming a state. This reflected the way in which many of the oldest European nations had been formed in the past, but times had changed and things did not work out as planned. These two countries (Yugoslavia probably even more so than Czechoslovakia) did not possess the common ethnicity, history and national myths which were needed to achieve homogenisation or cohesion in a new nation. At the time, Slovaks in Czechoslovakia and Slovenians and Croats in Yugoslavia realised that this was the best they could hope to achieve and that their quest for full national independence could not (yet) be successful. After all, the new states did represent protection against German and Hungarian nationalism, which had been of major concern to the smaller nations for a very long time.

All in all, Europe in general looked quite promising in the 1920s. Unfortunately, the Communist revolution in Russia brought a new and previously unknown factor into the politics and society of Europe. Marxist academic ideas became flesh where they were least expected, in a country that had not yet become an industrial society. Vulgar Communism, as practised in Soviet Russia, looked savage and totally alien to most people in the rest of Europe. For outsiders, it certainly added to their perceptions of the 'otherness' of Eastern Europe.

There has been much debate why Communism took roots in Russia first. Some say that the Russian (and more generally the Slavic) soul is somehow more susceptible to collectivist ideas and that Russians were for ages used to the iron fist of their Tsars. Much as they detested it, so the argument goes, they also secretly admired it, and it was not difficult to have the Romanov Tsars replaced by a Communist Tsar – Stalin. The alleged taste of the Orthodox Church for grandeur and for a strong nation-state is also supposed to fit into this picture. There may also be some weight in the argument that a country as large and sparsely populated as Russia is difficult to govern, and therefore needs a strong centralist government. Lenin was smart enough to realise that the utterly impoverished Russian peasantry (and the relatively few industrial workers in the country) would, at least initially, back any change. He also had the support of Germany, which saw benefit in anything that would make Russia weaker. Once the revolution was carried out, only the monstrous machinery of totalitarianism was able to maintain the system in place and any dissent had to be quashed at the level of mere thought.

But the situation was not much different in the other two totalitarian systems, Nazism and Fascism, that were produced by industrialised Western Europe during its worst ever economic crisis, the Great Depression. Nazism and Fascism had elements in common but they came into existence in the very different social settings of Germany and Italy. The latter country was much poorer and its southern regions were, socially and economically, in a state of near feudalism. What was common to both was the attempt to solve the internal problems of a nation through military expansion, justified by a dangerous nationalistic or even racial ideology. Much more affluent than the Soviet subjects though the majority of them were, Germans and Italians also appeared susceptible to totalitarian ideas and were unable to rid themselves of dictatorship. There was something in these three political ideologies of the twentieth century that was radically different from the logic of any previous system of governance or any previous war for territory. The consequences were perhaps comparable only with those of religious wars and the persecution of heretics in the past, although even these never went to such extremes.

Today we are aware of the intrinsically evil nature of Nazism and Fascism but that was not yet the case in the 1920s and the 1930s. Initially, Hitler's and Mussolini's ideas were debated in perfectly respectable circles and had advocates all over Europe, even in democracies like Britain where Mosley's British Union of Fascists was formed. In the beginning, some of their social and economic ideas were accepted as legitimate contributions to the debate about solving the deep problems of Europe at the time. The ultra-nationalistic and racial aspects of the two ideologies were apparently not taken seriously enough. Anti-Semitism had long been present in Europe, even in its most affluent parts, and needed only to be inflamed to result finally in the unspeakable horrors of the Holocaust.

The new states of Eastern Europe and their societies were not particularly unusual in their reactions to these developments: some were more sympathetic to the new ideologies, some less. Eastern Europe did not then exist as a political concept but the geographic Eastern Europe was split into two groups. The first consisted of pro-Western countries, linked to France and England, the second, of pro-German/pro-Italian countries. Each of these countries was hoping to obtain security guarantees ahead of the forthcoming conflict, which soon seemed inevitable. Some, such as Hungary, began to slide towards their own form of nationalism, hoping perhaps to recover the pride and the territories lost in World War I. Czechoslovakia, Poland and (at least initially) Yugoslavia pursued a policy of thoroughgoing friendship with the Western Allies. They were very aware that they would be the first targets of Nazi and Fascist expansionist politics, as indeed they were. Despite this, the West adopted a policy of appeasement towards Hitler and, in the Munich accord of 1938, sacrificed Czechoslovakia, the richest and most developed democracy of what was then Eastern Europe. 'A quarrel in a far-away country between people of whom we know nothing', are supposedly the words used by the British Prime Minister Chamberlain to dismiss the problems in Czechoslovakia and to justify his deal with Hitler.[43]

During the inter-war years, Czechoslovakia was, in many ways, a model country. It had a functioning democracy, a good economic base and an educated population. It had a pro-Western foreign policy but its leaders, Masaryk and Beneš, were not hostile at all towards the Soviet Union. In fact, the country leant more to the left than to the right. The only stain on its record was the way the Czechs looked down on their much poorer relations, the Slovaks (who had previously been discriminated against by the Hungarians), and did not take seriously their wish for full equality in what they wanted to be a federal country – at least this is how the Slovaks saw the situation. During the war this helped to push the Slovaks into the arms of Germans.

Poland was less a model democracy and more a 'learning democracy' as a friend of mine, a Polish historian, describes it. Although there was a parliament and there were political parties, the country was effectively run as an authoritarian state, although not one of a right-wing, nationalist nature, under the leadership of Piłsudski. The country was predominantly rural, with a weak middle-class, and it had many more economic problems than Czechoslovakia, not least because it had reconstituted itself out of three very diverse parts which, for almost 150 years, had belonged to three different states (Russia, Prussia/Germany and the Austrian Empire). In addition, the Polish state did not treat its Ukrainian minority fairly and had territorial disputes, a major one with Lithuania and a smaller one with Czechoslovakia. Domestic politics in this period centred on the conflict between the left and the right; foreign policy focused on averting the menace from both the Soviets and the Germans. Poland signed treaties with both powers. Despite this, Stalin and Hitler attacked and partitioned Poland in 1939, making it very difficult for

---

[43] As quoted in Adrian Hyde-Price, *The International Politics of East Central Europe* (Manchester University Press, 1996), p. 22.

Poles to decide which of the two neighbouring states that invaded them was worst. (Some Poles, fleeing Soviet and German troops in opposite directions, met with one another in the middle of their country.) For this reason, liberation by the Soviet Army in 1945 was met with very mixed feelings by Poles, even more so because the Soviets went on to eliminate the elite of the non-Communist resistance movement (in the Katyn massacre and by other means), thus making room for a new Government which was to their liking. Indeed, the Soviets also got rid of a number of the less amenable Polish Communists.

The Baltic states gained independence while caught between Germany and the Soviet Union. Latvia and Estonia were internationally recognised in 1921. Lithuanian independence was only won after a bitter row with Poland, which held on to Vilnius the capital of Lithuania. In 1940, the country was occupied by the Soviets as part of an agreement with Nazi Germany. It was then overrun by the Nazis and once again occupied by the Soviet Union. It only regained its independence in 1990. The fates of Latvia and Estonia were similar. In 1940, Soviet Union also started a war against Finland (which could easily be described as an Eastern European country, given its geographic position and its relationship with Russia!) and that country was forced to surrender some of its eastern territories. Bordering neutral Sweden on the west, Finland's main worries about security concerned the Soviet Union, not Germany. Following its experience in 1940, Finland sided with Germany (although it was far from embracing Nazi ideology) and declared war on the Soviet Union in 1941, as did Hungary and Slovakia and (later) Romania. In the whole Baltic area, countries were obliged to reach some kind of compromise with Nazi Germany. In some cases – although this was not true everywhere – compromise involved taking part in oppression of the local Jews, a reflection of the desperate position of these small countries caught between Nazi Germany on the one hand and the Soviet Union on the other. (The French Vichy police, in much less dramatic circumstances, assisted in the deportation of Jews and there were cases of collaboration with the Nazis in other Western European and Scandinavian countries.) For the Baltic states, devising a policy that accommodated the demands and expectations of Nazi Germany became a matter of life and death for their own nations. The ethical question – what is the right balance between protecting the life of one's nation and refusing to endanger the lives of other fellow human beings? – remained relevant. Many European nation-states do not exactly have a record in such matters that can bear too much examination[44]. What is important though, is that the modern Eastern European nations do distance themselves from any wrongdoings in the past, and join the collective European memory of the Holocaust.

With all its internal problems, Yugoslavia, the other creation of the Paris Peace Conference, was not a model country at the time but it was no worse than any of its neighbours. Italy turned Fascist and was openly hostile towards Yugoslavia, hoping to get control of the eastern Adriatic coast. Hungarian nationalism was radicalised and the country drifted towards the Axis powers. In Austria too, sympathies were with Germany. A dictatorship was imposed in 1933, the prime minister was assassinated the following year and the country was annexed by Nazi Germany in 1938. In the circumstances it faced, the Yugoslav leadership tried to please Hitler without compromising itself too much. It acceded to the wishes of the Axis powers under the condition that the country would not be drawn into the war. This might not have been the noblest position to adopt but it was probably the best Yugoslavia could do. Nobody either could or wanted to offer it a meaningful security guarantee, and the Yugoslav Army was far too weak to stand alone against almost any of its neighbours. Despite all their faults,

---

[44] 'Since 1945 the term "collaborators" has acquired a distinctive and pejorative moral connotation. But wartime divisions and affiliations often carried local implications altogether more complicated and ambiguous than the simple post-war attributions – of "collaboration" and "resistance" would imply… In France and Belgium, and also in Norway, resistance against the Germans was real… But not until the very end of occupation did the number of active resisters exceed the numbers of those who collaborated with the Nazis out of belief, venality or self-interest.' Tony Judt, *Postwar: A History of Europe since 1945*, William Heinemann: London, 2005, p.33.

Yugoslav politicians of the time tried to be pragmatic. However, the 1941 military coup d'état, which had what appeared to be wide popular support (and British backing), changed everything and enraged Hitler, who attacked Yugoslavia in April of that year.

Hungarian domestic politics during the inter-war years essentially consisted of a conflict between moderate conservatives and extreme nationalists. The loss (largely to Romania) of about a third of the Hungarian ethnic population and two-thirds of the country's former territory after World War I deeply influenced its foreign policy. Germany seemed the only country to have some understanding of Hungarian grief over these losses so, when the conservatives lost control of the extremists, Hungary turned openly pro-Fascist and joined the war on the side of Germany, regaining parts of Slovakia and Yugoslavia.

Romania greatly benefited from Hungary being on the 'wrong' side in World War I and received the large province of Transylvania in the peace settlement. In 1923, it adopted a new constitution, boasted to be one of the most democratic in Europe at the time. Economic development was heavily dependent on domestic oil production: in 1937, Romania was the second largest oil producer in Europe and the seventh largest in the world[45]. But like Hungary, on the eve of World War II, Romania turned to the extreme right in the hope that it might regain territories lost after World War I through its participation in war against the Soviet Union. It only changed its position in 1944. Bulgaria leaned to the Axis powers as well, although it is also known that the Bulgarian Tsar, Boris III, resisted pressure during the war to deport Bulgarian Jews. In Greece, a conservative dictatorship was established in 1936 but, in 1940, the Government rejected Mussolini's call for surrender. The country was then attacked and occupied by Germans and Italians.

---

[45] http://www.presidency.ro/?_RID=htm&id=1

In summary, those Eastern European countries that did not side with Germany suffered enormously. The additional problem for them was that, because of Nazi ideology, Slavs were treated much worse by the Germans than, say, the French were. For that reason, losses in Eastern Europe were far greater than anywhere else in Europe. (This includes the colossal human sacrifice made by the Russians.) For example, in Slovenia, 5.4% of the population was killed during World War II and in Poland 16%[46]; in Britain that percentage was 0.6%[47] and in France 1.35%[48].

Europe of the post-war period, and its collective memory and identity, is based on the experience of Nazism, Fascism and the Holocaust. Generations of Europeans (excluding those in the neutral countries of Ireland, Spain, Portugal, Sweden and Switzerland) have been brought up knowing about the importance of the lessons for the future that their parents and grandparents learned from the experience of Fascism. For all but extreme right-wing groups, this remains unquestioned. But Western Europeans did begin to question their parents' views of the Soviet Bloc and Communism at a very early stage. During the post-war period, left-leaning public opinion in Italy, Germany and (above all) France showed a persistent and almost religious trust in Communism of the Soviet type. And since Communism could at least be shown to have its origins in benevolent humanist ideas, which Nazism and Fascism could not, obvious parallels between the three ideologies, at least when it comes to the numbers of their victims, have

---

[46]

http://en.wikipedia.org/wiki/List_of_World_War_II_casualties_by_country#Casu alties_by_country

[47] John Corsellis, Marcus Ferrar, *Slovenia 1945 – Memories of Death and Survival after World War II* (IB Tauris 2005). This book is also suggested reading for those interested in the issue of reprisals against anti-Communists in Eastern Europe after World War II.

[48]

http://en.wikipedia.org/wiki/List_of_World_War_II_casualties_by_country#Casu alties_by_country often been rejected[49]. Consequently, attempts to recognise the experience of totalitarian Communism as a part of the shared memory of Europe were not met with the enthusiasm that they deserved[50].

Part of the reason for this was ideological: there was a new and substantial leftist electorate in Europe after World War II that was sympathetic towards Communism and which dismissed reports about what was really happening in the Soviet Union as propaganda. This electorate thought that, at worst, there was a correspondence between American influence in Western Europe and Soviet influence in Eastern Europe. (This is a belief that is still alive and well in some quarters of post-Communist societies.) The other reason for the sympathy was that (Soviet) Russia, as the driving force behind Communism in Eastern Europe, had also been an indispensable ally against Nazism that paid

---

[49] The author does not subscribe to the view heard occasionally in Eastern Europe that all three totalitarian systems 'were equal'. In fact, the three cannot easily be compared as they did not emerge simultaneously in the same countries, and they were also of very different duration. Comparison may be more valid between, say, Franco's regime in Spain and Tito's regime in Yugoslavia. Another difficulty in comparing the different systems arises from the fact that, although there were periods of violent anti-Jewish campaigns in the Soviet Union and also massive movements of entire ethnic groups which amounted to little less than genocide, Communism was not, by and large, racist in its ideology. What the author does advocate is that seen from the perspective of an individual (Eastern European) nation, Communism was a central experience that, in some places and with some people, even occasionally overshadowed earlier memories of Nazism and Fascism, the ones which remain the primary historical memories in the West. Cumulative numbers suggest that Communism, in its various incarnations, has been responsible for greater numbers of killings of its opponents worldwide than the other two totalitarian systems. If nothing else, this shows the profound appeal of Communist ideas to people of all races, which nonetheless resulted in large-scale oppression.

[50] Norman Davies says: 'On the ideological front, Westerners are accustomed to thinking of the Second World War as a two-sided conflict, of good fighting evil. The Soviets had a similar dialectical view. They were the authors of the concept of anti-Fascism, which caught on in the West, encouraging the illusion that all opponents of Fascism were inspired by similar values. In reality, Soviet communism was every bit as hostile to Western democracy as it was Fascism...' From *Europe East and West,* Jonathan Cape, 2006, p.246.

an enormous death toll for the victory, a toll that many Russians today see as being forgotten in the West's criticism of the Stalinist past.

Of course, Stalin, always well aware of this leftist sympathy in the West, seized the opportunities offered to him, not least because Nazi Germany became a very serious, real and direct threat to Russia. With the advent of Communism, Russia's consistent strategic interest in Eastern Europe, which went back to the time of Peter the Great, was revived with the missionary zeal of the Communist revolution. To be fair to the Soviets, it should be said that Stalin was also afraid that right-wing or otherwise hostile governments in some Eastern European countries could facilitate German attack on Russia, which eventually, as we saw, was exactly what happened. Hungary, Romania and Bulgaria hoped that siding with Germany might give them back territories lost in the aftermath of World War I. Poland, the Baltic States and Finland were, above all, frightened by the prospects of Russian invasion. (Finland had an added reason for its fears: it knew how appallingly the Finns that remained in the Soviet Union were treated.) These countries did not want to be protected from the Germans by a Soviet occupation.

Unfortunately, the Soviet Union did not hesitate to address its own security concerns first, even to the extent of signing a treaty with Nazi Germany at the expense of the smaller countries sandwiched between the two great powers. In addition, one must not forget the eagerness that still existed for the export of revolution: even before World War II, Moscow, through the so-called Comintern, controlled Communist and other anti-fascist movements all across Europe, not just in Eastern Europe. When war between Germany and the Soviet Union eventually broke out, Moscow hoped that the fight against Nazism, and also the common Slavic roots, would make it much easier to install Communist or at least leftist governments in Eastern Europe. Cynically, one might say that Eastern Europe got rid of the Nazis in four to five years, but it fell under Soviet control for fifty years. Eastern European fears of what the Soviet Union might do came true.

Initially, however, in 1939, the impoverished and unprepared Soviet Union signed the well-known Ribbentrop-Molotov treaty, and Moscow urged local Communist parties in Eastern Europe to refrain from armed resistance against the Nazis. In parts of Slovenia, for example, German troops were greeted by cheering mobs, organised by the Communist party, and World War II was portrayed by the Communists as a conflict between the equally imperialistic capitalist powers of Germany and Great Britain. It was not until the German attack on the Soviet Union in April 1941 that Communist parties around Europe were ordered to begin armed resistance. A part of Communist tactics to build up resistance movements was the idea of the so-called National Fronts – loose coalitions of all political parties that were willing to engage in resistance against the Nazis. These were meant to gain broad public support for resistance movements as well as for the Communist parties, which were ordered by Moscow to assume the pivotal and exclusive role in these Fronts – at gunpoint, if necessary.

Central Soviet strategy was not always successful and local parties occasionally acted against the expectations of Moscow. In Poland, there was a strong resistance movement that was not associated with the Communists. In Slovenia, Communists assumed the leading role in the resistance and did so by physically eliminating many of those who wanted to fight against the Nazis and the Fascists but did not want to be associated with a Communist revolution. This created impossible, almost absurd situations in which the anti-Communist side even asked the occupying forces for arms in order to protect themselves from Communist 'terrorists'; the Communists then accused the anti-Communists of treason. Even today, this is still a source of controversy among historians and ordinary people in Slovenia and elsewhere.

The British and Americans, realising that the Soviet Union would have to be brought into the war to beat Hitler, were ready to trade Soviet influence over Eastern Europe for Soviet military involvement. As early as 1943, in Tehran, Churchill and Roosevelt consented to Stalin's territorial request for the Baltic States, eastern Poland and Bessarabia (the eastern part of Moldavia). It appears that even Roosevelt downplayed the sinister nature of Moscow's demand for a zone of influence over Eastern Europe, and considered such a demand legitimate. Part of the Soviet argument, as described above, was that some of the Eastern European countries were hostile to the Soviet Union and were ready to allow the transportation of German troops across their territories. But the Soviets acted just the same in Czechoslovakia which was pro-Russian and leftist. In acting as he did, Roosevelt was ignoring the advice of military observers in Moscow, mistakenly thinking that Russia would democratise itself soon[51]. But it was Churchill who, on a visit to Moscow in October 1944, proposed spheres of influence in Eastern Europe to Stalin on a piece of paper. This is how Churchill describes the meeting in his own memoirs:

> At ten o'clock that night we held our first important meeting in the Kremlin... The moment was apt for business, so I said, 'Let us settle about our affairs in the Balkans. Your armies are in Rumania and Bulgaria. We have interests, missions, and agents there. Don't let us get at cross-purposes in small ways. So far as Britain and Russia are concerned, how would it do for you to have ninety per cent predominance in Rumania, for us to have ninety per cent of the say in Greece, and go fifty-fifty about Yugoslavia?' While this was being translated I wrote out on a half-sheet of paper:
>
> Rumania
>> Russia 90%
>> The others 10%
>
> Greece
>> Great Britain (in accord with USA) 90%
>> Russia (10%)
>
> Yugoslavia 50–50%
> Hungary 50–50%

---

[51] McCauley, p.11

Bulgaria
> Russia 75%
> The others 25%

I pushed this across to Stalin, who had by then heard the translation. There was a slight pause. Then he took his blue pencil and made a large tick upon it, and passed it back to us. It was all settled in no more time than it takes to set down.[52]

It may be that Churchill could not have imagined that what he himself later called the Iron Curtain was going to be so devastating for the nations to the East of it, although he must surely have had detailed reports from Moscow about how Communism worked in practice. But one cannot escape the impression that, just as Chamberlain had been prepared to turn his back on Czechoslovakia, Churchill considered Eastern Europe a worthwhile sacrifice for the greater good – victory over Nazism. One could also come to a further conclusion: that such horse-trading would probably have not been possible had the image of a *lesser* Europe not already existed in the Western European mind.

The famous Yalta meeting in February 1945 confirmed the Soviet influence over Eastern Europe. But the clauses in the Yalta Treaty, which concerned the composition of provisional governments in Eastern Europe, were, at least in the case of Poland, differently interpreted by Churchill and Roosevelt on the one hand and Stalin on the other. While in Czechoslovakia there was genuine, large-scale public support for the local Communist party (though not for its future dictatorship), in Poland and other countries in Eastern Europe the Communists were only able to come to power because of Soviet support and manipulation or, as in the case of Yugoslavia, because of the dominance that the Communists forcibly imposed on the resistance movement.

---

[52] Winston Churchill, *Triumph and Tragedy* (Houghton Mifflin, Boston, MA, 1954) as cited in McCauley, p. 116.

Thus while the British and Americans (with some help from the various resistance movements) liberated Western Europe and helped restore democracy there (even in Germany), Eastern Europe, with the exception of Yugoslavia, was liberated by the Soviets. Once their military presence was established, the Soviets certainly had no desire to help to restore the institutions of liberal democracy that *had* existed, however imperfectly, in most Eastern European countries before World War II. Instead, Soviet puppet governments were established that were even obliged to refuse the generous offer of the American Marshall Plan for the aid and reconstruction of Europe.

Ravaged by Nazism and Fascism, Eastern Europe did not enjoy its freedom long. In fact, within a few months or, at most, a couple of years of liberation from Nazism and Fascism, the region was forced into a new totalitarian system. In most countries, the shell of the national state remained (except in the Baltic countries which were annexed by the Soviet Union) but it was empty of freedom and of prospects for the future. Soviet-style Communism spread all over Eastern Europe, the Iron Curtain was drawn, contacts with the West were cut and the region sank into oblivion. In the eyes of Western Europeans, the region was labelled once again an alien, inhospitable, almost non-European place. It would remain so until the late 1980s.[53]

---

[53] Norman Davies wrote: '...historians have a problem. Somehow they must find a way of describing a complicated war in which, after several twists and turns, the combined forces of Western democracy and Stalinist tyranny triumphed over Nazi Germany... At the same time, without minimising the Western contribution, they must emphasise that Stalin's triumph had nothing to do with freedom and justice, and that by Western standards the overall outcome was only partly satisfactory. It is a tall order. To date, no one has succeeded.' Quoted from *Europe East and West,* p. 248.

The Communist Effect: The Creation of Eastern Europe

During the inter-war years of 1918 to 1939, the majority of Eastern European countries had a chance to experience independence and parliamentary democracy for the first time. True, they did not pass the test with top marks. Czechoslovakia was the only truly functioning democracy. But Poland and Yugoslavia had their good moments and some form of parliamentary life. Not all was doom and gloom. Economically, the region was not doing badly. The GDP of Czechoslovakia was 3,042 dollars per person in 1929, compared to 3,699 in Austria, 5,503 for the UK and 4,710 for France. Even without taking into account the fact that the less developed Slovakia was pushing down the Czechoslovak average, the total figure was higher than in Finland (2,717), Ireland (2,824), Greece (2,342), Portugal (1,610) and Spain (2,739) and was about the same as Italy (3,093). Poland (2,117) and Yugoslavia (which had an average figure of 1,364, although there were great regional differences) also fared worse[54]. Central Europe was still lagging behind Western Europe, but it was keeping it in sight. The same could not be said for Eastern Europe proper: Maddison's estimate for Russia in 1870 is 943 dollars and 1,386 dollars for the year 1929. After achieving a per capita GDP of 931 dollars in 1870, Romania slowed down after World War I and only reached 1,152 dollars in 1929. In the same period Bulgaria progressed from 840 to 1,180 dollars.

Some countries in Eastern Europe turned openly totalitarian in this period. This largely happened as a result of what they considered to be the unsolved issues from World War I. But overall, the record of Eastern Europe in this period was certainly not worse than that of Western Europe. In Eastern Europe, it was impoverished Russia which

---

[54] Figures are from Maddison, the comment on differences within Yugoslavia is mine.

produced Communism. In the West, Germany, affluent and industrialised, and Italy, the cradle of Roman civilisation and European art, produced two totalitarian systems, Nazism and Fascism, and brought untold suffering to millions. Only Britain, Ireland, France, Switzerland, the Benelux countries and the Scandinavian states preserved democracy during this period. Spain and Portugal too were ruled by authoritarian regimes. Socio-economic deprivation resulted in totalitarian systems both in the East and the West.

If it had not been for the Communist rule that began after World War II, the eight countries from Central and Eastern Europe that joined the EU in 2004 would probably not be referred to as Eastern Europe today. As I have attempted to show in previous chapters, Eastern Europe did not exist politically before World War II anyway. Looking at it from a hypothetical viewpoint makes it much easier to understand what Eastern Europe is not – a politically homogenous unit, a place destined to remain poor and in social disarray. Had there been no Communism imposed in Eastern Europe, these countries would most likely have further boosted their economies, strengthened their democracies and perhaps even joined the EU much earlier. On the eve of World War II, Slovenia and, above all, Czechoslovakia probably had the most mature economies of all Eastern European countries and would have probably gone on to have the potential to meet EU requirements at much the same time as some Western European countries did. (Although would there have been a European Union had it not been for World War II?)

As we know, history travelled down a different path. At the end of the war, generously helped by the presence of Soviet troops, Communist parties came into power in all the countries behind the Iron Curtain, thus consummating the agreement on spheres of interest between the great powers, and effectively creating what we have known ever since as Eastern Europe. Sometimes this happened through (more or less manipulated) elections, sometimes by threats and blackmailing of democratic politicians who gradually left or were removed from the political scene.

In Yugoslavia, there was a more indigenous form of Communism, legitimised above all by the Communist-led partisan resistance movement. Tito violently eliminated or skilfully discredited other political competitors and was recognised by the Allies as the local coalition partner. Later on, because of the 'fifty-fifty' agreement, Tito was allowed to play Stalin in his own backyard. This did not mean that democratic standards were any better in Yugoslavia. Quite the contrary: the immediate aftermath of the war was marked by the summary executions of political opponents. Tens of thousands at least, and probably many more, Yugoslav anti-Communist troops are believed to have perished in massacres in the dense woods of south-east Slovenia, near Kočevje and elsewhere, in the early summer of 1945. By some estimates possibly as many as 200,000 died, some of whom were handed over to Yugoslavia by the British Army either by force or under the pretext of being moved to Italy after they had fled to Austria. Sixty years later, Slovenian historians and forensic scientists are kept busy discovering hundreds of illegal mass-graves and the national psyche has not yet come to terms with what happened. Such pogroms were largely kept secret at the time but local Communists attempted to legitimise them by smearing anti-Communists as Fascists and collaborators with the Nazis. (Some of them actually were but they represented a very small minority.) In Slovenia, anti-Communists effectively committed political suicide when they allowed themselves to be forced into what they termed 'technical' collaboration with the occupiers (something that, as I pointed out earlier, happened in Western Europe too). These people were usually also the most pro-Western patriots, who hoped that Slovenia was going to be liberated by the British and the Americans, not by Communist partisans or, even worse, by the Soviets. While they were waiting for the Western forces to land on the Adriatic shores of Istria, the Communist partisans (who had an unspoken fear that British and American troops would land) were recognised by the Allies and, not long afterwards, the British handed the anti-Communist troops over to the Yugoslavs. The great powers had neither the time nor the will to attempt to understand the complexities of the politics of small nations that were already destined to fall into the Soviet zone of influence.

Most of these anti-Communist troops lost their lives in the woods of the Kočevje area in south-east Slovenia, an area already mentioned in connection with the fate of the Kočevje Germans. But there is more to the story. One day in 2005, I received a call from one of the English mourners at Karl Lavrenčič's funeral (described in the prologue) with whom I had been friends for years. An acquaintance of his, named John, had approached him and asked for his help in finding out more about his father. He had only a very vague idea that his father had been born in Yugoslavia. He had died some years ago in a small town somewhere in England and left few things behind which might have enabled his son to trace his life story. One of only two papers he left was his birth certificate, which indicated that he was actually born in Austria. At least this is what the name of the birthplace, written on the birth certificate in the distinctive German alphabet, appeared to suggest. The other document left was a sort of identity card issued by the Yugoslav Royal Consulate in Munich soon after World War II. But that was all there was.

It soon appeared that the German name on the birth certificate actually referred to a village in the Kočevje area which, at the time of John's father's birth, was part of the Austro-Hungarian Empire. Furthermore, with the help of church and government archives, it was possible to establish other family details, including a most surprising and unexpected one. John had a half-brother in Slovenia. Another family tragedy, quite typical of Central Europe in the years after World War II, began to unfold itself in front of our eyes. John senior, probably loosely associated through his wife or family with the ethnic German community in the Kočevje area, decided to flee Slovenia/Yugoslavia. What exactly prompted him to do so, we do not know. We can only speculate about the kind of threat to which he had been exposed, one that was frightening enough to make him decide to leave his wife and children. He never spoke about them in the new life that he had

110

established in England. How exactly he got to Britain also remains a mystery. Did he use any of the same methods that Karl Lavrenčič and Ljubo Sirc did? No one seems to know. John junior only remembers that his father talked about Yugoslavia and Tito with fear in his eyes, and warned his (English) children never to venture into that country. He died in the 1970s, but John junior visited the Kočevje area thirty years later, where locals showed him the few stones that were left of what was once one of the flourishing villages of the Kočevje Germans – the birthplace of his father.

The small provincial town of Kočevje that John visited in 2006 was already much changed from earlier times. Sixteen years ago, being on the edge of the restricted area, it was still very much a Communist stronghold, a dull and grey town as many across the Communist world were. Yet different shades of grey could be found across Eastern Europe at the time. The Communist systems imposed after World War II had much in common but, across the region and over the decades in which they existed, they were not all exactly the same. The Hungarian uprising of 1956 and the Prague Spring of 1968 were able to take place because of the strong, liberally minded middle-class which existed in these countries (at least in their capital cities) and which had a pre-war tradition of democratic life. In Poland, the Catholic Church enjoyed relative freedom because of its strong traditions and its major importance in the country. In the Baltic countries, their formal inclusion in the Soviet Union was, in fact, an annexation and it was followed by a mass immigration of Russian-speakers, with the purpose of changing the ethnic structure of the populace. Resentment against the Communists there was therefore focused on the ethnic/national issue.

In Yugoslavia, which was, apart from Albania, the only country of the former Communist bloc that was not in the Warsaw Treaty (i.e. was not under Soviet rule), the Communist regime was generally believed to be softer. In 1973, Tito was even proposed for the Nobel Peace Prize by some Western politicians. Yet his Yugoslavia had prisons full of

111

political opponents of various shades of opinion and even a concentration camp on a barren Croatian island. In fact, this notorious Goli Otok camp was set up precisely when Tito decided to break with Stalin (or vice-versa), as he wanted to imprison those of his political opponents who were the most faithful to Stalin and therefore, in one sense, perhaps the most genuine Communists. Hundreds died there in the most dreadful circumstances. Tito's dictatorship can probably be best compared with those of General Franco in Spain or General Pinochet in Chile but Tito, himself titled the Marshal, can certainly be held responsible for many more victims than these counterparts from the opposite side of the political spectrum.

How was one to live under Communism? As has already been said, it is important to understand that living under Communist rule in, say, Poland could be quite different from living under it in Hungary or Slovenia. While, for example, in Soviet-dominated Poland one was free to attend religious service, in Slovenia a teacher in a small town might prefer to attend mass in a nearby city in order to avoid bullying at work. And Christmas was not a public holiday in Slovenia as it was in Poland even though the country was almost equally overwhelmingly Catholic. The experience was also different at different times during the Communist dictatorships. A joke about the Communist government could earn you years in prison in 1950s Slovenia but, in the 1980s, it would cost you a fine or, at most, a conditional sentence. People from different Eastern European countries and of different ages could give different accounts of Communism but, just to provide an example, I will tell the story of my own family.

My father's father was born at the end of the nineteenth century in a village that is today 25km from the Italian border, not far from the village of Vrhpolje, which I mentioned in Chapter 1. He was born as a citizen of the Austro-Hungarian Empire. In World War I, he served in the Austrian army and, during a battle in the Tyrolean mountains, he lost half a leg. As a result, he had to give up hopes of taking over the family farm and instead he went to Ljubljana to be trained as a watchmaker. There he met his future wife and returned to a small town near his native village. By then, he was a citizen of the Italian Kingdom, as Italy got a chunk of western Slovenia as a reward for turning its back on its former ally, Austria during, World War I. (This is how Vrhpolje, together with the famous battle at Frigidus, ended up in Italy.) A few years later, the Fascists came into power in Italy and life became difficult for Slovenians there[55]. The Slovenian language was banned from public use and the church became the only place where it was tolerated. Fascist militias ravaged villages in the wider Trieste/Trst region, molesting the local Slovenian population: during one such expedition, a Slovenian musician was forced to drink machine oil until he died. There were documented cases of Italian teachers spitting into the mouths of children that dared to speak Slovenian in school. Four members of the secret Slovenian resistance movement were executed. This was probably the first antifascist movement in Europe and, in 1938, it came close to assassinating Mussolini at Kobarid, site of the famous World War I battle known as Caporetto in Italian.

In such circumstances, one of my uncles decided to become a priest. For him and for many of his fellows this seemed to be the only way to serve his nation in a public role. In 1944, my uncle was ordained a priest and was sent to a small village up in the hills. Italy had just capitulated and the Germans took it over. He managed to manoeuvre skilfully between the occupying forces, the increasingly authoritarian and ideologically exclusive Communist-led resistance and the anti-Communist movement, each of which came knocking at his door, some in broad daylight and some under cover of darkness, but all asking for his loyalty.

---

[55] Fascism inspired the then little-known Slovenian writer Vladimir Bartol to produce *Alamut*, a fascinating story set in medieval Iran and depicting a militant religious sect. The work, which is above all a criticism of totalitarian systems and ideological violence, was rediscovered in the aftermath of 9/11 due to its prophetic account of Islamic fundamentalism and terrorism. In 2005, the book was included by the Spanish daily El Pais among the 50 greatest works of historic fiction and is available in English as well (Scala House Press, 2004).

At the end of the war he was allowed to go for postgraduate study in Rome but, after a delightful year there, the Yugoslav authorities revoked his exit visa. Life was becoming more and more difficult for the clergy and for the Church faithful. Under pressure, he joined the association of priests that was organised by the regime itself but he could not keep his mouth shut. On one occasion, during a meeting of this organisation, he stood up and complained about the lack of religious freedom. Not long afterwards, he ended up in jail as a Vatican spy and stayed there for six and a half years, involved in construction work on the new housing developments that were being built in the new Yugoslavia.

At home, my father's family supported the (Communist-led) resistance movement during World War II without knowing much about the Communist agenda behind it; for Slovenians in the Italian-occupied areas, national liberation took precedence over any other considerations. Even so, after the war, the family was put under surveillance because of my uncle's activities. My father left teaching because of the pressure and went on to become a dentist.

My mother's family ran a relatively large farm in central Slovenia, near what was then the border between Yugoslavia and the Italian kingdom. During World War II, the family largely supported the resistance movement led by the Communists but some of the extended family joined the anti-Communist forces. For this reason, two of her uncles lost their lives in the post-war massacres. After the war, despite their support for the resistance, large areas of the family estate were confiscated. After graduation, she married my father and came to live in a small town in western Slovenia, half an hour's drive from the Italian border.

Politics was often discussed in our home but we soon learnt to live double lives. In school, we had to join in the praises of the resistance movement, the Communist Party and Tito. Religion, let alone politics, could not be discussed at all – even the word Christmas could not be mentioned. On Christmas Eve we all went to the midnight mass but we still had to go to school the next morning. Father Christmas and St Nicholas (St Claus) were banned; only the Soviet-inspired Father Frost was allowed down the chimney.

In secondary school, I was the best student among 1,500 and yet, as I was privately told by one of the teachers, because of my religious belief I was not even formally proposed for what were called Tito scholarships, aimed at the ablest students. It was not a big deal for me at the time but all those who think that Yugoslavia was substantially different from the rest of Communist Europe should know that this was still happening in the early 1980s. In 1986, I was a conscript in the Yugoslav Army in Sarajevo. I was bullied because of my religious beliefs and, together with the other conscripts, I had to attend Marxist classes. I still remember the half-educated officer who said that Yugoslav guest-workers in Germany might well live better than in Yugoslavia but the product of their labour was alienated from them, which was not the case with the happy workers who stayed in the country.

Of course, not everyone in Slovenia (or, for that matter, in other Eastern European countries) felt the same way about the Communist system as my family did. As well as those who were obviously corrupt, there were many people who, because of family tradition or for other reasons, sincerely believed in the system. Among the Party members there were some genuinely honest people. And then there were the kinds of pragmatic individuals that are found in every society, who simply adapt to the situation, never raise their heads above the parapet, never speak up and just want to get by. It is important to realise this in order to understand that the return to democracy in the 1990s was not greeted with equal enthusiasm by all strata of society. I am not just speaking here of Party apparatchiks but also of a number of people who simply got used to the system and were not particularly interested in change, especially if it meant uncertainty about their jobs or the availability of affordable housing. For the system was not totally bad. There was work for all, a free quality health service and affordable social housing.

In 1960, the GDP of Yugoslavia was 2,437 dollars per capita. In Austria it was 6,519, in Italy 9,719, in Germany 10,839 dollars. It was 3,072 in Spain, 2,956 in Portugal, 3,146 in Greece and 4,282 dollars in Ireland. Yugoslav average GDP was, however, lower than that in Bulgaria (2,912), Hungary (3,649), Poland (3,215) and, of course, Czechoslovakia (5,108 dollars), and only higher than that in Romania. Twenty years later, the average Yugoslav GDP was 6,063 dollars. (For comparison: Irish GDP then was 8,541 dollars, while the Czechoslovakian average was only a little bit less – 7,982 dollars.) According to estimates done by Ljubo Sirc, the classmate from the prologue and a former professor of Economics at Glasgow University, the Slovenian GDP was about twice the Yugoslav average. This means that, in the post-war period, the Czech lands and Slovenia were seriously lagging behind the core of Western Europe, but were at about the income levels of Spain, Portugal, Greece and Ireland until these countries began to fully benefit from their EU membership.[56] However, the difference between Eastern and Western Europe became very serious after the 1980s. For 1990, the estimate for GDP for the Czech Republic alone stood at 8,895 dollars and for Slovenia 11,404. At the time it left Yugoslavia, Slovenia was richer than Greece (9,988) and Portugal (10,826) and it was almost at the level of Ireland (11,818 dollars), all measured in Maddison's 1990 international dollars. Eleven years later, in 2001, Slovenia's GDP (in the same units) was 13,843 dollars and the Irish GDP was 23,201 – such was the dramatic success of the Celtic Tiger in the EU and, on the other hand, the cost of transformation in Slovenia!

---

[56] The estimates are taken from Ljubo Sirc's book *Iščemo podjetnike* (GV, 1996), in the Slovenian language.

For Yugoslavs there was also free foreign travel: from about the 1970s, we had this unique possibility of travelling freely abroad, as much as we wanted. When Yugoslavia opened its borders with what was then Western Europe, Slovenia, bordering on Italy and Austria, profited the most. Slovenians were the lucky ones in the Communist world, being able to travel abroad whenever and as often as they liked. Shopping in Italy or Austria was a fortnightly occurrence. We looked for the products that were not easy to find in the then Yugoslavia or were cheaper abroad, such as imported fruit, bathroom tiles or fashionable clothes. But it did not end with shopping. Books on politics that were banned in Yugoslavia, and printed by ethnic Slovenian publishing houses in Italy and Austria, or by political exiles in the USA or Argentina, were often hidden in the boxes of washing powder that were brought back across the borders on shopping expeditions. In other words, Slovenians were looking for all those artefacts of material, cultural and spiritual normality that their fathers and grandfathers knew in earlier times. The re-emergence of democracy and independence in the 1990s, and the accession to the European Union in 2004, therefore, represented a return to the normality of previous generations, not a venture into entirely uncharted territory. While other countries of the former Communist bloc were not as lucky in terms of travel abroad, the desire for such artefacts of normality was the same, even if they did not have the same opportunity to indulge in it. They still had the possibility of listening to short-wave BBC radio programmes, to German Deutsche Welle or the Voice of America. I myself have warm childhood memories of the Slovenian ethnic minority radio programme from Trieste/Trst.

The other very important aspect of the open Yugoslav border was trade. Slovenia, the only Yugoslav republic bordering Western Europe, which had a relatively strong industrial tradition from the time of the Austro-Hungarian Empire, benefited the most. It became the greatest Yugoslav exporter and the richest Yugoslav republic – and probably also the wealthiest nation in the whole Communist world. It was precisely because of the opening of the borders and the slightly less rigid Yugoslav economic system that we left the Czech Republic behind during the post-war period. But, as our macroeconomic data were hidden in the Yugoslav average, politicians and political scientists were caught by surprise when, after 1990, Slovenia suddenly emerged as the richest of all the new independent states. This is another example of how flawed the analysis of Eastern Europe was and sometimes still is.

Returning to the subject of shopping abroad, Trieste/Trst suddenly became a consumer Mecca for Yugoslavs[57]. This city, tucked in a short stretch of Italian territory under the Kras plateau, started to make a good living out of Yugoslav shoppers. For those on a budget, there was a particular part of the Trieste/Trst centre, around the old marina, where every imaginable type of Asian-made cheap good was on sale. The place, called Ponterosso, attracted scores of Yugoslavs, particularly from the southern parts of the country, who were easily recognised by the large plastic bags they carried to their cars and buses. Although they were fuelling the local economy (this was one of the reasons for the lack of enthusiasm for a democratic and independent Slovenia among some in Trieste/Trst, for whom it meant a loss of business), their shabby image made them targets of contempt for local right-wing groups. These became even more convinced of their racial superiority over the 'Slavs', a term they indistinguishably called Slovenians, Croats and all other Yugoslavs in the Trieste version of the 'Eastern Europeans' label.

Turning to the East, Slovenians did not always know much about the rest of Eastern Europe. If you travel from Slovenia to Hungary today, you can still see the remains of barbed-wire installations on the Hungarian side, the kind of fences that did not exist on the Yugoslav border with Italy or Austria. Other Eastern Europeans needed special

---

[57] Similarly, after the fall of the Berlin Wall, and the opening of the border between Austria and Slovakia, Hainburg and Parndorf, two rather insignificant little towns on the Austrian side of the border, acquired a similar function as a shopping Mecca for Slovakians.

permission to go on holiday to the Yugoslav (Croatian) coast. (I am told that often the permission excluded at least one member of the family who had to stay at home as a guarantee that the others would return!)

'Eastern Europe' was a good bargain for Yugoslavs in those times, and long weekends in Prague or Bratislava by coach were very popular. People brought back large quantities of fine Czech china and other goods. Sadly, the price difference was a result of the economic decline that the Czech Republic suffered under Communism. As a country which possessed a thriving economy before World War II, the Czech Republic was very badly hit by Communist economic policies when compared with other nations that had been less successful in the interwar years. Its fate alone proves how disastrous Communism was.

In the era of the Austro-Hungarian Empire, strong links existed in particular between the Czechs and the Slovenians, but all this was completely gone in a generation or two. We became strangers to each other. My first trip, to what we too called Eastern Europe at the time, came in the late 1980s. I was an active member of the Slovenian Catholic student movement then and we responded to an invitation from a similar group in Krakow, Poland[58]. We drove in a Yugo, a Yugoslav/Serbian-made car of the day, via Hungary and Slovakia, and we were subjected to meticulous screenings of the car at each border crossing. In Poland this was after the period when martial law had been imposed but it was still a time of tense relationships between the police and the public. The country appeared poor and things like meat were very difficult to find. There was still a hint of the old glamour of the great historic city of Krakow. We splashed out in a fancy restaurant in

---

[58] Catholic and also centre-right political movements in the whole of Eastern Europe were at the time heavily influenced by their Austrian counterparts. Austria, a relatively small and also a neutral country, has played a central role in the transformation/transition process in Central and Eastern Europe – a noble role that was very well rewarded by a significant share of the privatisation cake in the region. Lately, Austria has been replicating this model of economic influence in south-east Europe.

the city centre that was only accessible to a few. But, on the other hand, civil society was alive and well. Intellectuals and students were meeting in private homes or in semi-private offices and cafés to hold lively discussions about every possible political issue. Writers and other intellectuals were spearheading democratisation in all Eastern European countries – this was almost a cultural revolution. I had not seen such things happening on the same scale in relatively well-off Slovenia. There, a much more sophisticated socialist regime cleverly supported members of the generation that had succeeded the one which created Tito's revolution, letting them indulge in post-modern, experimental and marginal arts, hoping that this would prevent the return of a 'reactionary' mainstream art and civil society.

There is one more concept that needs to be included in a full picture of Eastern Europe – that of the diaspora; the emigrants. As mentioned earlier, many anti-Communists of different colours – like Karl and Ljubo from the Prologue, or John's father – fled Eastern Europe during the years of Communism. Because these were usually highly-educated people and patriots, they soon established ethnic associations and even political parties and shadow parliaments in exile. The Slovenian political emigrants in Argentina, smeared as traitors by the Communist authorities, developed an impressive system of schools, crèches, companies, publishing houses, radio stations, etc – all in the Slovenian language. Scores of third-generation children speak fluent Slovenian after sixty years of exile. (Poles all over the world have created even larger and more influential ethnic communities.) By the nature of things, these were, of course, people of staunch conservative or Christian Democratic views (as well as some liberals) but it is true that it was only within the ranks of European Christian Democrats that they found partners in the West who would listen to them. In fact, the organisation of Christian Democratic parties even set up a committee to deal with the issue of Central and Eastern Europe where exiled politicians had the opportunity to meet Western politicians and lobby for their cause. (In the early years of the Cold War some of these exiles were also useful to the Western intelligence services.) In the late

1980s, many of them – by then growing old – served as links between Western politicians and government officials on the one hand and the new democratic political establishment that was emerging in Eastern Europe on the other. Ljubo Sirc, for example, used his connections with Liberal International to help the newly-emerging liberal party in Slovenia to develop. These political emigrants did not, however, always find their homeland very welcoming. They were vigorously opposed by former Communists, who labelled them as traitors and extremists, but even the new democratic politicians sometimes found their presence embarrassing. They saw them as out of touch with the local situation, and harbouring expectations of what the new democracies could deliver that were too high. In many cases, the exiles – often as a consequence of persecution, imprisonment or even the execution of family members – bore terrible scars and the result was long-lasting frustration.

In Yugoslavia we also had another category of emigrants, the so-called guest-workers, who, in the 1970s, began to be attracted to Germany and, to a lesser extent, to Austria, Italy, Switzerland, France and Sweden. Just as some Irish went to the UK, it became customary for some Yugoslavs to travel to Germany for a couple of years to work (as a builder or nurse, for example) and then to return home. Many did so and invested the money they earned in a new house or a small independent business. The remittances they sent home also boosted the Slovenian economy. When these guest-workers were travelling home for the Christmas holidays and there were long delays at the Yugoslav border-crossing, the media traffic reports always referred to them returning for the 'winter' holidays – the word 'Christmas' could not be mentioned on the radio.

In the meantime, Slovenia developed to such an extent that it started to need a foreign workforce itself, above all in construction and services. From the 1970s onwards, buses of workers from Bosnia, Kosovo and other parts of the former Yugoslavia came pouring into Slovenia, in much the same way that 'Eastern Europeans' have done into Ireland

and the UK recently. (In 1962, the GDP per head in Slovenia was 195% of the Yugoslav average but only 37% in Kosovo[59].) In addition to our own economic emigration to Germany, Slovenians also got to learn about economic immigration. The workers from other parts of Yugoslavia were not always received warmly. There was a degree of xenophobia, though not the concern about loss of jobs that troubled some in Ireland and the UK when faced by a similar immigration. In the Communist system people thought of jobs, taxes and state expenditure as God-given, something you could not lose – or change. Because Slovenians can just about understand the Croatian and Serbian languages, the immigrants often did not make the effort to learn Slovenian properly. This all added to the sense of a danger to Slovenian identity within the Yugoslav state. Yet, in the 1990 referendum on the independence of Slovenia, the majority of immigrant workers, by then well settled in their new country, voted in favour of it, very well aware that their home republics would not be able to offer them more than Slovenia did. With few exceptions, around 200,000 were given Slovenian citizenship (out of a total population of 2 million). A similar issue concerning Russians who moved into the Baltic countries after World War II proved much more complex.

Slovenia appeared to be moving on despite Communism. Still, the net real incomes in relatively affluent Communist Slovenia only reached 1939 levels again in 1957. Because of the political and economic crisis in Yugoslavia, after the death of Tito in 1980, incomes fell further after 1988 and thus, in 1991, were not much above pre-World War II levels[60]. One can imagine that the situation in the more isolated economies of Soviet-dominated Eastern Europe was even less rosy.

In 1956 and 1968, Budapest and Prague respectively rose against the inhuman face of Communism. Both revolutions were quashed by

---

[59] Ben Fowkes, *Eastern Europe 1945–1969, From Stalinism to Stagnation* (Longman Pearson, 2000), p. 92. A similar estimate was produced by Ljubo Sirc.
[60] See note No. 22.

Soviet tanks[61]. (As a response, Yugoslav ideologists developed the concept of 'Socialism with a human face'. What is good about unadorned Socialism, one might ask, if it needs to have a 'human face' added to it?) Some more positive signs came with the cautious normalisation of relations between West Germany and East Germany at the beginning of the 1970s. Then, in 1975, the permanent Conference on Security and Cooperation in Europe (now called the Organisation for Security and Cooperation in Europe[62]) was established in Helsinki. Eastern European countries also joined it (they were allowed to do so by Moscow) and this marked the beginning of an easing of Cold War tension. Yugoslavia, which was not a member of the Warsaw Treaty and had been conducting a separate and independent foreign policy, then launched the non-aligned movement, composed of mainly left-leaning third-world countries with Yugoslavia and India as the leaders. Romania too was allowed a degree of independence in international affairs, perhaps because it was deemed strategically less important for Moscow[63].

Encouraged by the (rather timid) human-rights agenda of the Conference on Security and Cooperation in Europe papers, Czechoslovak political opponents, led by Vaclav Havel, founded the Charter 77 movement. Three years later, the economic difficulties in Poland reached their height and the Solidarity movement was founded. General Jaruzelski declared martial law after six months of protests, allegedly to prevent Soviet invasion. This was also the year of Tito's death, which was soon followed by troubles in Kosovo and then by the Yugoslav debt crisis. In 1989, Solidarity won the elections and formed a Government, triggering democratisation movements all over Eastern Europe. Led by intellectuals, above all writers and former dissidents,

---

[61] For the comparative economic study of fringe European countries it is interesting to note that some of the Hungarian refugees who, after the quashed uprising found shelter in Ireland, were taken aback by the living standards of late 1950's Ireland.

[62] www.osce.org

[63] Gökay, p. 20.

people filled the streets and squares, demanding change. This process took different forms in different countries across the region and took different lengths of time to run its course, reflecting local differences. But it is important to note that, in almost all places except Romania and Yeltsin's Russia, it was a completely peaceful process. Eastern Europe, as a political reality created by Communism and the Cold War, began to fall apart.

The Growing Pains of Transition

The democratisation process in Eastern Europe in the 1990s also represented an opportunity for the restoration of national sovereignty. In the case of the Baltic states, and the states of former Yugoslavia and Slovakia, this actually accompanied the process of democratisation. In fact, regaining independence was sometimes more attractive and emotionally stimulating than the much more demanding task of building a democracy. As we saw earlier, the years between 1918 and 1939 witnessed the first attempts in the majority of Eastern European countries to establish a nation-state. This meant that they were already lagging behind countries in Western Europe, even though Italy and Germany had only emerged as nation-states themselves in the late nineteenth century. Given the consequences of World War I, the economic crisis of the 1930s and the rise of violent totalitarian systems, it is not surprising that the mere twenty years or so between the two world wars were not enough to allow these new nation-states and their democracies time to consolidate their positions. After World War II, there was another chance but this time national sovereignty was limited by the Soviet Union and/or Communism.

A new opportunity arose after 1990. But in the meantime, societies in the West had begun to talk about life beyond the nation-state, which finally led to the creation of the European Union. In such a context, the new patriotism in Eastern Europe after 1990 was difficult to comprehend. It appeared out of touch with the spirit of the time in the rest of Europe. The drive to establish new nation-states by those small nations that had not had the chance to do so earlier in their histories was often misunderstood in Western Europe as an expression of a will to fragment, a movement towards what has been portrayed as Balkanisation (one of those political terms wrongly associated with the

Balkans[64]). The counter argument – that only sovereign nations can decide on joining transnational or intergovernmental organisations like the EU – did not sound strong enough, both because the world had moved beyond traditional concepts of sovereignty and because most of these nations had only very limited experience, if any, of being a sovereign nation.

Nevertheless, with some exceptions, most of the new states from Central and Eastern Europe, once they joined the EU, became some of its most devoted and enthusiastic members. There is a good reason for that: for the peoples and Governments of Central and Eastern Europe the enlargement of 2004 was not (only) an enlargement of an already existing union. For them, it was a re-creation of a more wholesome Europe, one which cannot exist without them, a return to the realities before Yalta and the Iron Curtain. It was also a confirmation of their essential European virtues and qualities. Before World War II, life in cities like Ljubljana, Prague, Budapest, Bratislava and Warsaw (as I have been trying to show throughout this book) was not substantially different from life in Vienna, Munich, Milan and Berlin. There were differences in the size and wealth of the cities, but the way of life and the mentality of the people were essentially the same. This is too often forgotten.

Even the late Pope John Paul II, in his last book *Memory and Identity*, spoke about Central and Eastern Europe, and challenged the notion that these countries 'returned' to Europe after the fall of the Berlin Wall. 'An injustice has been done to Poland,' writes the late Pope, 'and to the Poles by the misleading thesis of a "return" to Europe'. Among the arguments in favour of the claim that the Poles (and, by analogy, other peoples in Central and Eastern Europe) have always been there

---

[64] Maria Todorova in *Imagining the Balkans,* Oxford University Press 1997, notes that the term was not coined in the context of the Balkan nations' struggle for independence from the Ottoman Empire, but when the Austro-Hungarian and Russian empires fell apart and this resembled the disintegration of the Ottoman Empire. (See pp. 32–35.)

as a part of Europe, the Pope lists the early adoption of Christianity, the Polish contribution in wars against the Mongols and later the Ottomans, various Polish philosophers and, more recently, the Polish contribution during World War II. Poland was more courageous than the Western Allies, the Pope argued: 'While the Western democracies deluded themselves into thinking they could achieve something by negotiating with Hitler, Poland chose to accept war, despite the clear inferiority of her military and technological forces. At that moment the Polish authorities judged that this was the only way to defend the future of Europe and the European spirit.' As we saw with the villagers of Vrhpolje, Eastern Europeans often resort to history in defending their position in Europe. This is not because they would like to live in the past, but because they want to draw attention to the fact that in the past both parts of Europe, East and West, used to live one shared history, not two separate ones.

In the eyes of Eastern Europeans, the last two generations of Western Europeans have become too easily accustomed to thinking of themselves as Europeans in an exclusive way, even though neither Western Europe nor even the European Union can simply be equated with Europe. On the other side of the divide, Eastern Europeans never stopped thinking of themselves as Europeans and did not start thinking of themselves as Eastern Europeans until the Western Europeans told them that that was what they were. But, in reality, Eastern Europeans are not Europeans because of their interactions with Western Europe, but because they too are the heirs to Europe's Judaeo-Greco-Christian-Humanist culture. Obviously, the ways in which this culture was adopted were different in Eastern Europe as a whole and in the various nations within it. (There were also differences in the ways European culture expressed itself in Italy and in Britain, in Spain and in Sweden.) But that does not make Eastern Europe less European.

It is also true that in south-east Europe and 'Eastern Europe proper', the late arrival of Enlightenment ideas resulted in the slower development of the economy and liberal democracy, but even that does not make these countries less European, only less Western European. The Enlightenment is primarily a legacy of Western Europe but the European legacy as a whole cannot be reduced simply to the Enlightenment. This is what the draft European Constitution attempted to do (and failed).

Western Europe has not yet become accustomed to its newly-discovered sister and has not yet adopted her legacy in the joint and common heritage of Europe. In addition to the Latin and Greek scripts, the Cyrillic script is also a part of Europe's inheritance; the whole Orthodox spiritual and artistic tradition belongs to Europe in the same way as Humanism and the Enlightenment do. Eastern Europe's tragic experience of Communism should become a part of the continent's collective memory, not just a grievance in conservative circles in Eastern Europe or an ongoing frustration for the disenfranchised. In culture, Tolstoy, Dostoyevsky, Sienkiewicz, Milosz, Kundera, Andrić, Ionesco, Bartok, Smetana, Dvořak, Plečnik and Jančar are some of the most widely recognised and valued Eastern European artists and yet they are still missing from many textbooks across Western Europe. We have the term 'robot' because of a Czech novel. We owe key astronomical discoveries to Copernicus, a Pole, and the very fundamentals of modern electricity were laid down by Nikola Tesla, a Serb from Bosnia-Herzegovina. One of the latest models of the Volkswagen Passat was designed by Robert Lešnik, a Slovenian. Lech Wałesa, Vaclav Havel, Mikhail Gorbachev and Pope John Paul II are some of the names that have become a part of the vocabulary of international politics and fundamentally changed Europe in the twentieth century. And there would have been no Renaissance, and therefore no Humanism, without the Greek artists and scholars who fled Greece after the Ottoman conquest and settled in Italy, carrying with them the intellectual legacy of the classical world.

It would, of course, be false to deny that the great men and women of Western Europe outnumber those from the Eastern half of the continent. There are many reasons for this. The first is demography:

128

Eastern Europe has always been far less densely populated than Western Europe. Because of the difference in economic development which was a consequence of this, there were not enough large urban centres in Eastern Europe with the critical mass needed to encourage excellence in learning and science. If their talents were discovered at all, the most capable of Eastern Europeans simply had to leave for centres of learning elsewhere. These were mostly located in Western Europe where their origins were often forgotten or deliberately ignored. For many centuries, Slovenians, Czechs, Poles and others were simply labelled 'Austrians'. Consider, for example, the fate of Dr Friderik Pregl who received a Nobel Prize in 1923 for his discoveries in chemistry. Born as a Slovenian in Ljubljana at a time when there were only around 1.25 million Slovenians, he is usually cited as an Austrian scientist. Certainly he left Slovenia for Austria 'proper' when he was a young student and there are conflicting accounts of whether he himself felt Slovenian or Austrian, but the issue of identity would probably not have arisen for him had there been a Slovenian national state during his lifetime.

The two most notable exceptions to the shared legacy and collective memory of the two halves of Europe were probably the Ottoman conquest of south-east Europe and the fifty years of Communist (Soviet) domination in Eastern Europe. Since its fall, Communism has often been too easily dismissed and parallels have even been drawn between it and the benign American influence over Western Europe in the same period. One must not forget the differences between democratic and totalitarian political and social systems but there was also the economic factor which made the two influences (American and Soviet) very different. Because the Communist/Soviet domination came about in a period that was characterised in Western Europe by a historically unprecedented growth (also heavily stimulated by the United States), the whole of Eastern Europe missed out on a unique opportunity to boost its economy. This can be very well illustrated by the case of the Czechoslovakia. Before World War II it was the most developed of all Eastern European countries and its cars, made by the firm of Škoda, were among the best-built cars in the world. In 1950 its GDP per capita was still 3,501 dollars[65] (for Czechoslovakia combined); almost the same as Austria (3,706). Forty years later the Austrian GDP per capita was 16,905 dollars, while the Czech GDP was 8,815.

Since Eastern Europe was finally liberated, dignitaries and policy-makers, scholars and journalists, property developers and tourists from the EU-15 countries have often praised the progress that the new EU members from Central and Eastern Europe have made since the re-emergence of their independence and democracy, and have even congratulated them on how much they have done since their accession to the EU in 2004. They are right in a way, but the realities are much more complex: these countries did not come out of the blue on 1 May 2004, nor was their relative progress merely a result of their newly-acquired independence, democracy, market economy and EU membership. Let's turn back to the example of the Czech Republic. As it emerged out of Communism in 1990, its GDP (8,815 dollars) was only about a third lower than the Irish or Spanish or Portuguese GDP of the time, which ranged from 10,826 for Portugal to 11,800 dollars for Spain. Slovenia, which during the inter-war years caught up with the Czech Republic economically, came even closer with 11,404 dollars per capita. The Estonian GDP then was 10,794, the Latvian 9,886 and the Lithuanian 8,446. (Unfortunately, the three Baltic countries experienced a particularly dramatic fall in their GDP in the early 1990s, due to loss of markets, the complex relationship with Russia and the painful restructuring of their economies.) The stretch of countries from Estonia to Slovenia, i.e. the Central European tier of Eastern Europe, was clearly doing better than the rest of Eastern Europe, and these countries – despite Communism – were not dramatically poorer than the countries at other margins of Europe. In other words, the historic and geographic advantage of Central

---

[65] Figures are from Maddison and are in the so-called 1990 international Geary-Khamis dollars.

European countries could not have been wiped out completely by Communism. This explains the difference in performance between Central Europe and 'Eastern Europe proper', but also – at least in part – their ability to catch up after 1990 and, in particular, after their integration into the EU.

Further afield, the figures for 1990 differed. Bulgarian GDP was 5,597, Romanian 3,511, Yugoslav (as an average within pre-1990 frontiers) 5,279, Albanian 2,194. In 'Eastern Europe proper', Belarus GDP was 7,184 and Ukrainian 6,027. Both Ukraine and Belarus experienced a sharp decline in GDP in the following years. But the 1990 figures alone show that historic differences in economic development within Eastern Europe as a whole have persisted or – because of the accelerated growth in the west of the Continent throughout the twentieth century – even increased.

Unfortunately, many history and politics books on the subject treat Eastern Europe in a uniform way. This is particularly true for history before the nineteenth century and in the post-war period. Because of this they find it very difficult to explain the differences in the economic development that exist among the Eastern European countries, as outlined above. Even developments after 1990 are difficult to explain without knowing the past. Why are Estonians the boldest of all and Slovenians the richest, yet perhaps the most cautious as well? Why is Poland the most enthusiastic Atlanticist and why are conservatives there so strong? Why are the Czechs the most Eurosceptical and also probably the most liberal in the region? Why did some of the countries get rid of their former ruling elites, while, in others, faces from the past continue to dominate? Why have some Eastern European countries seen large proportions of their workforce migrating to Western Europe and others have not? Such questions cannot be convincingly explained without looking, not only at the past fifty years of Communism, but also at a slightly more distant past.

In the lead-up to the twentieth anniversary of the fall of the Berlin Wall, some of the new EU member states were found not to be terribly enthusiastic about the uniform plans for the celebration. They did not want to be seen primarily as victims of the Soviet Union, mercifully rescued by the West. True, their experience of Communism was common to all the countries of Eastern Europe, but they did not want their individual identities to be reduced just to that. And even in their experience of totalitarianism they were not alone: after World War II, Spain, Portugal and Greece endured right-wing dictatorships. Indeed, some of the developments in Eastern Europe have had surprising similarities with developments in these countries. Confrontation of a dark past, issues of reconciliation, social backwardness caused by totalitarian isolation, the lack of economic freedom, similar stages of economic development (think of the similarities in GDP figures presented earlier) – all of these are familiar problems in states that have suffered totalitarian government whether of the left or of the right.

Various explanations have been given for the fact that, economically and socially, both 'Eastern Europe proper' and south-east Europe, have lagged behind the rest of the continent. Some even think that Orthodox Christianity, in much the same way that it was once able to reach an accommodation with the Ottoman occupation, was also less likely to have irreconcilable differences with Communism. In truth, it does seem that there is some difference between how Western Christianity (Catholic and Protestant) on the one hand and Orthodox Christianity on the other see the person as a part of society. Even contemporary Orthodox theology renounces the idea of giving priority to social problems; it underlines that the human person is the prime existential issue. Only within the framework of the individual human soul can one also solve social problems. 'Man is making our society and all the institutions ill…'[66] The two struggles, for men's souls and for the

---

[66] Metropolitan of Nafpaktos Hierothes, *The Person in the Orthodox Tradition,* Birth of the Theokos Monastery, 1999, pp. 105–106.

improvement of society, should run in parallel, 'with priority given to the cure of man... Those who give priority to the social problems are unaware of the reality and are also possessed by a *Western* notion of how these problems are solved.'[67] In contrast to this, Catholic teaching went further and, relatively early, developed the concept of 'structures of sin', whereby an individual is not solely responsible for his or her actions, when these actions are the result of circumstances of social injustice which are inbuilt in the society. In such a situation, the individual is unable to act morally, i.e. against the sinful structures, which are forcing him to act in an immoral way. So the task of the faithful is not just to change one's own moral conduct. Everyone is asked to help change society too. Similarly, the more conventional Protestant traditions are, according to Max Weber's famous theory, responsible for the development of the enterprising spirit of capitalism and the wealth the latter created in the West[68].

Therefore, while there may be a grain of truth in assertions about cultural and religious differences between East and West, they do not take us very far or at least do not explain the whole story. By the same kind of argument, one could consider the Mediterranean character and the omnipresent, sometimes militant, Catholicism in Italy, Portugal and Spain, as well as the emergence of Fascist/authoritarian systems there in the past, as underlying reasons why this part of Europe has lagged behind other regions. (But then, Nazism took roots in a largely Protestant country and German Catholics showed stronger opposition to it than Protestants did.) Talk of 'the Mediterranean character' has a parallel in oversimplified talk of the 'backward mentality' in Balkan nations, which is supposed to be a result of isolation in remote mountain valleys. (In Switzerland, similar terrain appears to have produced very different results.) Even Communism itself cannot alone be blamed for this alleged backwardness. The difference, however, is that of all the totalitarian systems experienced by Eastern Europe (and

---

[67] Ibid., italicisation is my own.
[68] Max Weber, *The Protestant Ethic and the Spirit of Capitalism,* Routledge, 2002.

whereas Western Europe knew only Fascism/Nazism, most Eastern European countries experienced both that and Communism), Communism was the longest lasting and most all-embracing. It shook the very foundations of the economic system in ways that the other two totalitarian systems did not. This is why Communism was so devastating.

The history of nations is influenced by a number of factors: natural conditions, economy, the prevailing philosophy of the political system, past history, the quality of the political elites, international relations, size, etc. The causes of wealth or poverty in nations are also various. It appears that, for a nation to grow rich or poor, a complex array of historical, political, natural, ethnical, social and even philosophical factors is required to be in the right conjunction. Eastern Europe has no inherent tendency towards poverty and no monopoly on it, despite all those newspaper photos of horse-drawn ploughs that accompany articles on agriculture in Central and Eastern Europe. What is undoubtedly true, however, is that, at certain points in history, significant portions of Eastern Europe just failed to produce the right conjunction of factors needed to grow rich (as also happened in some fringe parts of Western Europe). The last time this happened was the moment when Communist regimes were established after World War II.

Still, Eastern Europe is not all doom and gloom. Some of the new EU member states have world-class road and Internet infrastructures and still enjoy enviable levels of almost free health and other social services. However, almost fifty years of Communism took their toll, and the economies and societies of the new member states still have some way to go to become as robust and as strong as their counterparts in Western Europe. It would be wrong to deny this: political turmoil in Poland, Hungary and even the Czech Republic in the last couple of years have reminded us of that, as did the serious difficulties Bulgaria and Romania experienced in dealing successfully with corruption, organised crime and poverty, before they could become 'full' members of the EU, without being exposed to condescension from at least some member states. The volume and complexity of the Communist legacy could be easily proved mission impossible to a highly experienced and well-equipped Western government, especially when it comes to getting the necessary political support for the changes required. From this point of view, Eastern Europe did it very well.

The most serious blow that Communism delivered, however, was not to the economy; it was to people's self-confidence[69]. Eastern Europeans are generally much more wary and watchful people. Sometimes you can identify an Eastern European by the way he or she reluctantly and shyly approaches a policeman or a shop assistant. Life in Western Europe is built on trust between people, on the assumption that people are, in principle, honest and trustworthy. Not so in Eastern Europe, where (at least in the past) an individual was treated with suspicion in most social situations. He or she could not be trusted as a matter of principle; their trustworthiness needed to be proved in advance. For all the talk about humanism, Communism saw the diversity of individuals as the greatest danger to its grand project. It is here where one should look for the roots of the lack of courtesy that foreign visitors sometime observe on the streets of Eastern Europe. The true message of Communism to an individual was unmistakable. The system treats you as a cog in the machinery of a society on its way to a perfect Communist world, so you treat other people like cogs too. And if I am not valued and appreciated as a distinct person but only considered as a replaceable cog, then why should I value my fellow citizens who share the same fate as cogs in a machine, and surely

---

[69] Koch and Smith in *Suicide of the West,* Continuum, 2006, also list among the six key features of the 'West' optimism and individualism, two traits that can loosely be identified with what I term self-confidence. At the root of optimism, Koch and Smith see myths of the autonomy of man, his essential goodness and the belief that creation is constantly progressing. Communism denies all these. An individual is only worthwhile as part of a collective. It is important to note, however, that both authors make it clear explicitly that the *West* in the title of their book also includes what is popularly referred to as Eastern Europe.

cannot be any better than me?[70] In Eastern Europe, a sort of lethargy could – and sometimes still can – be observed, a result of the inability to influence one's own fate. Jobs and social welfare used to be taken for granted, almost as God-given; there was little that one could do in Communist times to improve one's life and living standards. In such circumstances, everyday routine (so often praised in the Anglo-Saxon/Protestant tradition as a virtue) turned into a burden. It was nothing more than a tiresome exercise which bore little relationship to one's social standing and could do little to affect it. As a result, this exercise began to be performed shabbily and work was poorly done. Work, formerly praised so highly in the Communist world, became of very little true value. It became an activity to be avoided and the products of it, particularly those consumer goods intended for the general public, ended up as poor in quality. Individual consumers were not considered valuable enough to deserve good products.

Generations of Eastern Europeans that grew up after 1990 have been gaining self-esteem at a great speed, often through their rising purchasing power and the gadgets of modern life that they can now afford to have. (Even consumerism can be helpful to some extent!) And yet distrustfulness has been built into the system and into their souls. That is why the new member states of the EU still have to fight

---

[70] This has been very well explained by Roger Scruton. Although he is making the case for national loyalty, the lack of what he terms 'accountability to strangers' was a feature of Communist societies and continues to some extent to be a feature of societies in transition. Scruton says that, in the transition process, 'almost as soon as democracy is introduced a local elite gains power, thereafter confining political privilege to its own gang, tribe or sect, and destroying all institutions that would force it to account to those that it has disenfranchised.' To apply Scruton's argument to our discussion, one can see that many countries in transition have found it very difficult to take-off economically and in other ways because of an inherited mistrust in 'strangers'. Only those that one knows (fellow party apparatchiks, for example) are deemed suitable for a business project, as good civil servants or for political work. Others need to be excluded. In this way, the elites in Communist countries have replicated themselves in contemporary political, business and even civil service elites in the post-Communist era. See Roger Scruton, *A Political Philosophy,* Continuum, London 2006.

against a greater amount of red tape and why, despite what flashy government websites might claim, the spirit of enterprise is, in practice, not yet encouraged by a sufficiently flexible legal environment and by enough government initiatives. This lack of self-confidence – of which a lack of personal responsibility is a corollary – works together with the shortage of tradition of good governance and public administration to impede the development of an organisational culture and *esprit de corps* among civil servants.

The new political and economic system has unleashed the free spirit of enterprise, but this has certainly not been helped by the sad record of what has become known in Eastern Europe as 'wild privatisation', i.e. dubious, rigged privatisation, involving the use of insider information and a complete disregard for the position of the workers. In an often weak legal environment, this practice was usually possible because of the 'old-boys' network', i.e. the informal network of the business, political and even cultural elite from the Communist era which continued to hold power. To finance a (crooked) management buy-out, a manager, probably a former party apparatchik, would have a far better chance of getting a loan with a bank than a 'stranger' (in the sense used by Roger Scruton – see note 68). Often, the loan was guaranteed by the same shares which it had been used to buy and not by the manager's personal property. Such practices were also facilitated by the weak and dispersed ownership that could not exercise a proper control on the management. For their part, the former political elite often made sure that legislation provided a sufficiently vague legal environment to shield their friends in the business elite from potential domestic and foreign competitors. Often the politically attractive argument of 'national interest' was used to support the creation of such legislation. All this, of course, came at the price of financing the party political machinery that would return them to power every four years and thus help replicate the political elite. A survey of the various elites in the country, carried out in post-Communist Slovenia in 1995, has shown that the people who constituted the economic and cultural/artistic elite in that year were

89% the same as they were in 1988 before the changes. Only within the political elite was the equivalent figure lower – at 71%. The case was much the same in Hungary and, to some extent, in Poland, although in the Czech Republic the former elite lost almost all of the little credibility and legitimacy it once possessed[71].

In many societies in transition it took years before canny apparatchiks accepted normal ways of doing business and discovered that a good corporate culture is better – even for them – than murky business practices. (In the meantime, those playing by the rules suffered grave disadvantages.) Gradually, businessmen and politicians during the transition years came to look like responsible and respectable citizens, even in the eyes of foreign analysts and partners, who might embody the virtues of stability, predictability and the right yields.

But, for those who were looked down on during the Communist years, seeing the same people in power again is simply too much to bear. It has created frustration, augmented support for unconventional, often chauvinist, political parties and fuelled the kind of radical conservative emotions that put off foreign observers and analysts so much, and strengthened stereotypes about Eastern Europe as a socially backward, conservative, illiberal and intolerant place. The situation is only exacerbated by the slow and/or only partial (in some instances, non-existent) process of restoring property seized during the Communist regime. This also means that people, who, in their traditions and social views, were predisposed to once more become the middle-classes of the new societies, were often prevented from doing so. Instead, a new middle-class has been emerging out of the post-Communist circles, but these new rich are only slowly acquiring the attributes of such a class, above all its sense of social responsibility. Little or nothing has been

---

[71] See Anton Kramberger, *Positional Elites in Politics, Economy and Culture in Slovenia During 1988–95: Summary Statistics on Elite Segments,* CESTRA, 1998. For other countries see Frane Adam, Matevž Tomšič, *Transition Elites: Catalysts of Social Innovation or Rent-Seekers,* Faculty of Social Sciences, University of Ljubljana (unpublished).

done in Eastern Europe in terms of positive discrimination for the previously disenfranchised to compensate them for the fact that the legacy of the previous regime has allowed a small section of the population to achieve an (economic) advantage over everyone else. The political transformation has not taken things back to the beginning and created a level playing field for everyone. Such measures were believed to be impossible to implement.

More generally speaking, at the heart of the economic debate in countries in transition was the question of whether their governments should undergo shock therapy or should manage the change to a market economy in a more gradual way. The American economist Jeffrey Sachs was among those who advocated a rapid approach, and he was a frequent visitor to Eastern Europe. On the other hand, the Nobel laureate Joseph Stiglitz was very critical of this argument and he has been able to put forward the examples of Poland, Hungary and Slovenia as countries which took the less painful road of a gradualist approach that led to greater social and political stability and faster economic growth in the long term[72]. The advocates of shock therapy admitted that their approach does indeed lead to a drop in individual living standards in the short run but that this type of economic reform brings the promised gains later on. Using a graph with consumption on the vertical axis and time on the horizontal axis, they produced the so-called J curve, widely known in conservative circles in Eastern Europe. They have also argued that a gradual approach in post-Communist economies has benefited exactly those kinds of people described earlier: '[from] enterprise insiders who have become new owners only to strip their firms' assets; [from] commercial bankers who have opposed macroeconomic stabilisation to preserve their enormously profitable arbitrage opportunities in distorted financial markets; [from] local officials who have prevented market entry into their regions to protect their share of local monopoly rents; and [from] so-called local Mafiosi who have undermined the creation of a stable legal foundation

---

[72] Joseph Stiglitz, *Globalisation and its Discontents,* Penguin, 2002, pp. 180–188.

for the market economy.' These are the unintended winners in the transition process[73]. Such views may have a party political flavour, but not everyone in post-Communist societies would be happy with Stiglitz when he writes about former Communist businessmen as 'pragmatists who wanted to get ahead in the system. If the system required that they join the Communist Party, that did not seem an overly excessive price to pay.' He then continues: 'While some of these "practical men" were ready to steal as much of the state's wealth for themselves and their friends as they could get away with, they were clearly no left-wing ideologues... It had taken a long time for us finally to stop judging people by whether they were or were not Communists during the old regime – or even by what they did under the old regime.'[74] Looking at events from the outside, it is probably desirable to finally have names and telephone numbers of people with whom to do business in Eastern Europe. This may even be – in a long-term perspective – good from the point of view of the national economies there, provided that the stripped assets are invested productively, and not translated into lavish houses, cars and yachts (which is what usually happened). But innovative privatisation has created social tensions, has compromised both the market economy and democratic ideas, and ultimately created distortions in the markets, especially in the financial market, where small and medium entrepreneurs with no political friends were displaced by comrades in business.

Any approach to economic reform in Central and Eastern Europe obviously had its own political implications too. But another thing needs to be noted above all – and here both the radical and the gradualist reformers, each in their own way, are right. For a successful transition a country needs, above all else, well-functioning state institutions, a sound legal infrastructure, good laws and the agencies to implement and enforce them, truly independent courts and a

---

[73] Joel S. Hellman, *Winners Take All – The Politics of Partial Reform in Postcommunist Transitions,* World Politics 50 (January 1998), 203–34.
[74] Stiglitz, pp. 167–168.

professional civil service. Even the staunchest advocates of radical reforms would now agree with this. Slovenia and some other countries were only successful in their gradual reforms because they had better institutional infrastructures and not necessarily because of the gradualist approach itself. Moreover, the gradualist approach was perhaps successful in some countries only because these countries could afford it: they had relatively well-functioning economies, already exposed, at least in some degree, to market forces. Industries in these countries were better able to survive, with no major difficulties, in a fully-fledged market economy. People kept their jobs, taxes were paid, state coffers were filled, and a relatively generous welfare state was left almost intact and ready for those who remained outside the job market. It could thus be argued that Slovenia and other countries that opted for the gradualist approach could actually have afforded a more radical form of transition, because their economies and legal environment would have been able to survive this without additional major social costs. Paradoxically, some of the less-prepared former Communist countries listened to the advice of the shock therapists – and paid very high social costs. Once prices were liberalised and state-owned enterprises were privatised, non-profitable businesses closed down, the prices of consumer goods went up, and jobless people could no longer afford those goods, while the half-emptied treasury could no longer sustain the welfare state that once existed. The macroeconomic data may have looked fine on paper but it all came at a high social cost and at some cost to the new political elites as well.

To admit the truth, the new democratic political elites in Eastern Europe have not always lived up to their promises either. The first battalions of these usually consisted of uncompromising, often naïve idealists who had never run anything other than a literary society or a semi-illegal intellectual journal. (However, even the most experienced macroeconomists and policy analysts would probably not have been able to do much better in the circumstances.) What happened was that, all across Eastern Europe, a few years after the first democratic elections, pioneering democratic governments fell and were replaced by political parties which had been fancily re-branded either by truly progressive ex-Communists or simply by those who were less scrupulous and did not mind laying spurious claim to being Western-style Social Democrats or even Liberals.

Indeed, the 1990s were not the best of times for new political forces in Eastern Europe to arise from the ashes, after party political life had been so long frozen there in the decades after World War II. In the meantime, the party political scene in Western Europe had been through significant transformation. The left had become less radical (think, for example, of Joschka Fischer in Germany), perfectly respectable and politically correct. The conservative camp (the Conservatives in the UK and the Christian Democrats in the Continent) had mostly achieved their primary goals. Then, the oil crisis and the slowdown of the 1990s struck. People became less interested in low-tax policies and more in keeping their jobs and preserving a generous welfare state. The left understood all this well enough, while conservatives were busy thinking how – with birth-rates at a post-war low – to finance full employment and the same levels of social benefits. In this context, along came a newly-liberated Eastern Europe with its own economic problems which it was very poorly equipped to solve. The economic policies of the conservatives in Eastern Europe were often more suited to the post-World War II conditions of, say, Adenauer's Germany than anything else. Such policies were unsuitable for the kind of challenges that the Communist economies were posing. In addition, socially speaking, the policies of the conservative parties in Eastern Europe were indeed quite conservative, certainly more so than those of their sister parties in the West, and, for this reason, were not exactly attractive to an electorate that was eagerly embracing consumerism as fast as it could. Furthermore, the conservative parties not only wanted to change the whole spectrum of economic and social policies, and the fabric of society; they also wanted to address all the injustices done during the Communist regime – from annulling politically-motivated court rulings (such as the one in which Ljubo Sirc was sentenced to death) to restoring forcibly nationalised property (like the textile company that belonged to Ljubo Sirc's father). It wanted to compensate all the many people who had been disenfranchised by the former Communist regime. But the stakes were too high. It was much easier for the former Communists to simply adopt the appealing image and message of the contemporary European left. After all, the messages of the left at the time coincided to a great extent with the issues that were at stake in the East. The majority of Eastern Europeans were not primarily interested in compensation for injustices; they were more concerned about keeping their job and preserving relatively generous public services that were free for all. And the left did not ask for additional sacrifices from the public in order to reach the living standards and private incomes enjoyed in the West.

The profile of the new political landscape was also determined by the degree to which a country implemented 'lustration' – the removal from office of those who had been compromised by participation in the former regime. The former East Germany is known to have been most systematic in doing this. Others followed suit, with the intensity of the process being inversely proportional to the perceived softness of the former regime in a particular country. Generally speaking, throughout Eastern Europe, lustration was only half-heartedly implemented.

In some countries, the process of lustration also swept editors and journalists from their positions. Despite such measures, the return of democracy has not also meant the return of truly free and unbiased media. Old networks persist in some quarters, underpinned by the 'old boys' in the business who make sure that the chosen media get enough advertising – as long as they report and comment in the 'right' way. Certainly political pressure is being exerted on journalists and editors from both left and right, by the 'old boys' and also by the new political elites, but some of the journalists and editors are only willing to assert their independence from the one and not the other. In countries that enjoyed a softer version of Communism – so soft that it is politically more correct to call it 'socialism' – the bias, because of social and political inertia, is usually against the political forces that brought down Communism. The reason for this is that the most compromised journalists from the Communist era often retired from actual writing and moved into management and even ownership within the media business – such moves were, of course, only made possible with the help of the 'old boys' network' and the privatisation spree in the new market economies. From there, it was easier to control editorial policy, while simultaneously defending the 'independence' of the media. But the real independence of editorial policy in established democracies in the West is a result of decades or more of professional effort by journalists, of the competition of ideas and capital, and the demands of a democratic society. Where these traditions are absent or weak, because they were broken during the totalitarian era, 'independence' can at best be half-hearted.

Former Communists, sometimes assisted by new politicians, also succeeded in spreading doubts about parliamentary democracy. Superficially, there may be similar doubts in the long-established but disillusioned post-war democracies of Western Europe. However, the political parties there are not only held in check by their political adversaries but also by a powerful civil society which exists only in an embryonic form in the East. If lack of self-confidence reflects the worst damage inflicted by Communism at the level of the individual Eastern European, then lack of a well-developed and truly independent civil society reflects the most serious blow at the level of society in general: in a way, it can be described as society's lack of self-confidence[75].

Of course, even the former Communist regimes used to have what looked like a civil society from the outside: a number of organisations

---

[75] In the brilliant *The Geopolitics of Emotions* (Doubleday, 2009) Dominique Moïsi has this to say on national self-confidence: 'Confidence is as vital for nations and civilizations as for individuals, because confidence allows you to project yourself into the future... Confidence (distinguished from hubris) is one of the most important components of the world's health.' (p. 5–6).

from sport clubs, consumers' watchdogs and bee-keepers' associations to United Nation's clubs, arts councils, charity organisations and peace institutes. But local party members were always given the task of ensuring that the 'right' people chaired these societies, and the state was only generous in financing them as long as they were giving value for money, i.e. providing the illusion of an independent civil society. During the political transition, some of these organisations proved to be extremely useful as shelters for discredited former Communists. (In one Eastern European country, a former Communist party leader became the chairman of the National Olympic Committee. A few years later, now the representative of a non-state organisation, he was elected to the position of chairman of the board of the national television service, a non-partisan body, meant to be the guardian of the independence of the media.) Another useful role of these organisations was to produce all sorts of 'independent' and 'expert' opinions and reports to be used as political ammunition by the ex-Communists against their political adversaries. One has always to be careful in Eastern Europe when dealing with people who introduce themselves as 'independent' or 'experts' or both. In a society with young and only partially effective political institutions, experts are often – and falsely – seen as a panacea for all problems when, in reality, they often just provide a veneer of competent professionalism for decisions which have been made for political reasons. In addition, civil organisations and professional associations are still often established from above, by state or even party political initiative, and do not emerge from the grassroots.

Little valuable 'infrastructure' of civil society was already in place for the new political elite to use. There was no one to back them intellectually, never mind financially, and provide suitable independent expertise that would influence public opinion in their favour. As a result, they often appeared coarse, clumsy, off-the-mark, inexperienced, professionally incompetent and with no real support in civil society. Apart from writers' associations, the only organisation that they could occasionally count on was the Church, but even here the local situation varied greatly across Eastern Europe. In devout Poland, the Church was an important player and waved the flag for change. In the more secular Czech Republic, it was rather marginal. In Croatia, it was strongly on the side of the main new nationalist political party. Generally speaking, without the Church's support, there would not have been enough votes to elect the new political elites. This was certainly true in countries with a strong Catholic tradition, where the Church was not only the biggest single victim of the former regime but also its firmest opponent, nurturing a deep ideological/philosophical opposition to the very principles of the Communist system. This was perhaps not obvious to onlookers, but the liberal intellectuals who led the political changes in most of Eastern Europe (the situation was different in Poland) were rather out of touch with the conservative masses and they needed the Church to motivate people and bring them to the polling stations.

People in Eastern Europe have reacted to the changes of transition in many different ways. There are those who have never really trusted the new political parties and the changes that they have brought, and who remember the good old days with nostalgia, either because of the perks they used to enjoy or because their lives did not really change for the better (sometimes they became more difficult). This gave rise to support for various radical, extreme left and/or chauvinist parties, or for one of the reincarnations of the former Communist party. At the opposite end of the political spectrum, in the conservative camp, there are people who, whatever their present economic situation, continue to be staunch supporters of the new political parties, often those with a strong anti-Communist rhetoric. Except in Poland and possibly the Czech Republic, these are usually also the strongest supporters of membership of the European Union, which they see as a weapon against the former Communist elites. Then there are the new rich, who usually have strong connections with ex-Communists who have reinvented themselves as liberals. There is also a smaller group which consists of an emerging new centre-right political elite. Finally, there are those few who, after fifty years of leftist experimentation, still believe or hope for a genuine Social Democracy. This list is, of course, simplified and by no means exhaustive, because the political landscape in the new democracies of Eastern Europe is still changing. Parties keep forming, merging, splitting and going away; they change their names according to the current party political needs. Political parties are not always or not yet genuine intermediaries between the state and the individual in the political process. Party politics is often taken with deadly seriousness by the public and too lightly by the politicians. The public, especially the supporters of the new political parties, do not approve of tactical alliances with parties that have their origins in the former Communist elite or of any similar, pragmatic measures. For them, compromises are not acceptable, and everyday political choices are turned unnecessarily into major moral dilemmas.

In general, Eastern European politicians are in a much less secure position than those in the West. Party alliances are much more volatile and so is the luck of the ballot. People find it very difficult to plan their political future, and to choosing politics as a lifelong career is still relatively rare. There are few havens where one can spend time out of office. This is particularly true for the new political parties, because of the lack of 'infrastructure' in civil society.

If the political landscapes within Eastern Europe are varied, so too are its international relations. I explained earlier that Eastern Europe as a cultural concept was invented by philosophers and novelists in the eighteenth century, and that Eastern Europe as a political concept was really a product of the Cold War and Communism. It did not exist before World War II. In reality, since 1990 and, in particular, since 2004, the eight new member states of Central Europe have been taking quite distinct paths of domestic, economic, social and international development.

This is not surprising. Few political links developed between these states before World War II, and even those that existed lost international significance long ago. Moreover, some of the relationships among Eastern European countries in the inter-war period were rather cold; there were territorial claims and minority issues. On a cultural level, Czechs looked down on Slovaks and Poles, as their poorer neighbours. Slovaks enjoyed excellent relations with Poles, and the latter with Hungarians. Poles had a very bitter relationship with Lithuanians, and, of course, Russians. The Croatian-Serbian conflict was central to the Yugoslav kingdom. Hungarians were feared by Slovakia and Yugoslavia. Grievances existed between Romania and Hungary. But all these mostly stemmed from the fact that these countries were, for centuries, parts of others' empires, where state borders were not drawn along ethnic ones. Similar or greater animosities existed among Western European states too.

One of the frequent stereotypes of Eastern Europe today is that it resembles some kind of Tower of Babel. It requires patience to understand that ethnic minorities and the issues of ethnic identity were often manipulated or ignored in the Communist era and that, in some instances, they are only now coming to the fore. Sometimes this does not happen without tension or at least sensitivity on the part of either the minority or the majority population. But ethnic grievances also exist in Western Europe today after years of living with democracy. Think, for example, of Belgium, which is supposed to be at the heart of Europe. The only difference seems to be that, in Western Europe, ethnic identities are seen as a tourist curiosity (unless they pose a terrorist threat like they do in Spain). In Eastern Europe they are treated both as proof of the folkloric character of the region and as a potential source of conflict. Ireland and the UK needed decades to come together on the issue of Northern Ireland in order to stop violence there and, hatred and parallel communities still exist in the North. The conflict is probably no longer ethnic or may have never been entirely ethnic, but that is the case elsewhere too. In an affluent society, like that in Belgium, federalisation is an issue in the twentieth century, and occasional public references to a possible break-up make many Belgians extremely uncomfortable. Catalonia, the richest part of Spain, wants more autonomy and has now succeeded in its aim of recognition as a nation. My Italian friends tell me over the *pasta con tartufi* that, even after a hundred and fifty years of the Italian nation-state, not all Italians fully identify themselves with it. Austria is failing to implement its own constitutional obligations to the Slovenian minority in the province of Carinthia, where the populist nationalism of part of the German-speaking population is still blossoming in what is otherwise a very modern and, in many ways, exemplary Western European country. The situation with the Slovenian minority in Italy is similar. On the other side of the border, in so-called Eastern Europe, a much smaller Italian minority has a reserved seat in the Slovenian national parliament and a constitutionally enshrined veto on minority legislation.

The Višegrad community has been a modest attempt to build a new alliance of four Eastern European countries (the Czech Republic, Poland, Hungary and Slovakia), on the symbolic base of a much older, fourteenth-century agreement. It was encouraged by Western Europe which, at that time, thought the alliance could be both a laboratory to test the political maturity of EU hopefuls and, perhaps, a convenient waiting room for new democracies on the path towards real membership. In the Baltic Sea area, the Council of Baltic Sea States unites Estonia, Latvia and Lithuania with other countries in the region, mimicking perhaps the Hanseatic League[76], the old Germanic network of wealthy trading cities of the Baltic Sea. An older Italian regional cooperation initiative, Alpe-Adria, already included Yugoslav republics in the 1980s, and is now the breeding ground of a new and fancy Euro-region stretching from Milan to the Hungarian plateau. Since 1989, a number of Western and Eastern European countries have been incorporated in the regional organisation of the Central European Initiative, which partly resembles the old Austria-Hungary Empire, although its main driving force is Italy. But, generally speaking and contrary to assumptions that they constituted a unified political area, the new democracies of Eastern Europe, once they had satisfied their

---

[76] Price, p. 116.

main political, security and economic concerns through membership of the EU and NATO, did not recreate the single monolithic entity that some people (falsely) thought had existed during the Cold War. The Višegrad idea never came anywhere near matching the reality of the Benelux countries. Eastern European embassies are not housed under the same roof, as is often the case with the Scandinavian countries. With the accession of Romania and Bulgaria, diversity has only increased and there will be even more when the next enlargement of the EU takes place – whenever that will be. For the time being, concentric circles of EU states are being formed in the East, moving at different speeds. Those that are ready for the Euro or to join the Schengen Agreement and other forms of enhanced integration draw closer to the centre, leaving behind those that will need more time. With the accession of Romania and Bulgaria, there are now EU countries under a kind of supervised membership due to their lack of preparedness to fully assume all the obligations of the membership.

Western Europe made a mistake when the EU decided to have the 2004 enlargement done as a package. It was a mistake because it was falsely assumed that all eight countries (ten, if you include Malta and Cyprus) were essentially the same in terms of political, economic and social development, and that negotiating their accession as a package would therefore make things smoother for the EU. At the time of the enthusiasm of the early 1990s, Western politicians probably genuinely believed that a big-bang enlargement would impress the public in the West (or perhaps upset people less?). Quite the reverse happened: the sheer scale of the enlargement caused fear among the citizens of EU-15 in an already insecure world of fierce global competition, sluggish economic growth and terrorism. Voters in France and the Netherlands confirmed this in their referenda on the Constitution. In 2006, the Commission openly took the view that further enlargement would have to be put on hold, and it began to apply the criterion of 'integration capacity' which is, in reality, the controversial 'absorption capacity' in a new guise. The fact is that, after 1990, politicians failed to produce a genuinely positive vision of a united Europe and to inform their

150

electorates about the added value of new member states; too many have seen these new states as liabilities. Gone are the days of visionary politicians like Kohl and Mitterrand. Eight (or ten) countries joining at the same time, followed by Bulgaria and Romania, looked more like multiple trouble to many people in Western Europe than a celebration of diversity. The uninspiring conclusion was that these countries represented 21% of the new EU by population, but only 7% of the common GDP.

Moreover, the new (economic) nationalism, born in Europe after the failure of the Constitution and further encouraged by the financial crisis of 2008, is making new EU member countries even more wary. Also, hesitancy on the part of some of the EU-15 to open up their labour markets for workers from the new member states continues. (Recently, the EU-10 blocked the plan of the EU-15 to make it easier to hire workers from outside the EU, insisting that free movement of labour should be established within the EU first.) Not only is this contrary to the principles of the Four Freedoms of EU law and offensive to the people concerned, but it is also a sign that the societies of Western Europe are increasingly ailing. It highlights their identity crisis, their growing isolationism (scepticism about further enlargement is another sign of this) and perhaps also indicates a troubled relationship within the EU in years to come. It is a warning signal for new members.

What's next? Until recently, it seemed that the EU was already turning its attention to the Balkans and to 'Eastern Europe proper' – in other words to Belarus, the Ukraine, Moldova and Turkey. Well, this is certainly what the EU should be doing. But enlargement fatigue seems to be taking its toll. In insecure times, and because of lack of vision on the part of politicians, even the 2004 enlargement was greeted with doubts and mistrust in many of the EU-15 countries. This was despite the fact that few could point to real problems and the fact that enlargement fuelled economic growth across the whole of the EU. It is estimated that the enlargement has added 0.5% to the growth in the 'old' EU Member States annually[77].

The less than fully successful accession of Romania and Bulgaria made many negative perceptions worse and created two sets of victims. The first victims were the two countries themselves, because each began to be seen by some as a sort of second-rank member state. The second group of victims consisted of the countries in the Western Balkans. The rationale goes that, if Bulgaria and Romania were such trouble, then, surely, the Western Balkan countries will be an even bigger headache (something that is not necessarily true, as a comparison of many economic and social indicators would easily show). The enlargement process is thus now at serious risk of coming to a standstill. Fortunately for some, the Balkan countries have not really been performing well on their path to reform, and the rather poor annual Progress Reports, produced by the European Commission, have been a sort of relief to enlargement sceptics. There is, of course, no way (and rightly so) that these countries could hope for membership until they are ready; and it is difficult to see any of them, apart from Croatia, being ready by 2014 – the symbolically important 100th anniversary of the shots fired at Duke Ferdinand in Sarajevo which triggered World War I.

But the Western Balkans are badly in need of help, and leaving them alone now could result in much worse headaches later on. The truth about this war-torn region is that it does not itself possess the kind of self-motivation that the 2004 EU entrants demonstrated during their own negotiation and accession process. Some in the West therefore doubt if the Balkans are suitable for EU membership at all; here and there we hear ideas of offering the Balkan countries 'privileged partnership' status, and the same has been suggested for Turkey. Others believe that the EU needs to respond by adapting its approach

---

[77]See http://eur-lex.europa.eu/LexUriServ/LexUriServ.do?uri=COM:2009:0079:FIN:EN:DOC for a detailed assesment by the Commission.

and its enlargement strategies or face instability. An idea that has been floated is that countries of the region should be given the status of EU-candidates at an early stage, thus giving them a very tangible prospect of EU membership. At the same time, drawing them in to a very demanding negotiation process would constitute the right kind of pressure for reform, with the aim of affecting local politicians and civil servants. Politicians in the aspiring states would have a clearly-defined roadmap to EU membership and the public would insist that it was delivered on that basis. But such plans are not popular at the moment. In times of global economic crisis the priorities seem to be elsewhere. Superficially, it might seem right that they should be, but the EU will need to move on once the Lisbon Treaty is in place. The truth is that re-unification of the continent through enlargement of the EU – if sold to the public with political vision and courage – represents the best future that Europe could have and the only one that can give it lasting security.

Epilogue: The Future of Eastern Europe

What might Ruairi, whom you met in the Introduction, make of all this? And how can I help to ensure that sales of a flagship Slovenian product in the Netherlands do not go down once the Dutch become aware that the product was designed and constructed in 'Eastern European' Slovenia? It would be naïve to expect that Ruairi or his Dutch friends will start to read books about Eastern Europe and try to understand it. After all, how much do the English or the Dutch really know about the history of France, Spain, Italy or Austria? The difference is that they take the European nature of these countries for granted. This is not yet the case with countries from Eastern Europe. From the eighteenth century onwards, and above all for the last fifty or sixty years, people have been learning about Eastern Europe as if it was another world, one not fully European.

Perhaps low-cost airlines will do the job; they are the InterRail of modern times. The more (young) people visit Eastern Europe, the more it will begin to be seen as a normal place, and the more Ruairi will be able to refer to Poles, Czechs, Latvians, Lithuanians, Estonians, Slovaks, Hungarians and Slovenes individually, rediscovering the forgotten family of Europe, the more he will stop treating them as 'others' or lumping them together in one single indistinguishable tribe. By one more twist of historical fate, Ireland – at the fringe of Europe and with almost no historical links with Eastern Europe save St Ferghal – is perhaps in a unique position to deal with Europe's new 'Eastern Question', even though the recent economic downturn has driven thousands of Eastern European workers back home. However, by generously opening its labour market to Eastern Europeans, Ireland was, at least for a couple of years, a living social and economic laboratory for a new interaction between West and East. Furthermore, the political and economic history of Ireland was surprisingly similar to that of many Eastern European countries, and this similarity inspired many in Eastern Europe to emulate the Irish success story. Perhaps we need to revisit the political context of times when Ireland, Greece,

Portugal and Spain joined the Union to have a better understanding (and sometimes patience) of the recent and forthcoming enlargements.

However, the Irish experience will not be easy to replicate in Eastern Europe. It will probably be quite impossible to do it. Ireland has based its success on the coincidence of a number of factors. At the time it had decided to get rid of its isolationist and old-fashioned economic model, it already had a large pool of relatively well-educated young people (including women who had previously stayed at home) that were ready to take the jobs in factories opened by American investors. For the latter, the Irish connection, but above all the knowledge of English and relatively cheap labour, were the key factors in their decision to choose Ireland for investment. In addition, membership of the EU provided a large market for fine Irish meat and dairy products, rescued the countryside, and was instrumental in building the country's much needed infrastructure, above all its roads.

In contrast, the new EU member states from Eastern Europe have entered a much less generous organisation. In fact, they have not even been able to benefit fully from the Common Agricultural Policy; the alpha and omega of the EU we used to know: new member states were only slowly phased into the system, as the old ones were afraid that vast sums of money would disappear down an Eastern European agricultural drain. (The new member states may fare better with the regional funds, which are to remain a very important feature of the EU development policy in the future too.) American investments have, in the meantime, moved even further to the East, to the Far East, or stayed in Ireland because of the low taxes and knowledge of English. In addition, the societies of Eastern Europe are among the oldest in Europe, with birth-rates barely allowing for one-on-one replacement– or, in some cases, not even that. With the drain of their youngest and most talented people to the UK and Ireland, they cannot hope for a more prosperous future at home. Add to this the global financial crisis that hit the world at the end of 2008. New EU members' hopes that the momentum of years of exceptionally high growth rates will save them have been largely offset by the ripple effects of the downturn in their Western economic partners, above all in Germany, and by the lack of accumulated capital that Western countries still have in pension funds and elsewhere.

In summary, the Eastern Europeans are now much more on their own than Ireland was when it joined the Union (except perhaps for those like Slovenia and Slovakia which are already in the Eurozone). They will therefore need to reinvent themselves should they wish to build a better life at home. The goals for which they fought for so long – membership of the EU, NATO, the Eurozone and the Schengen Agreement – should now be seen as means to an end rather than final objectives. Eastern Europe needs to mature fully as a contributor to European security and economical stability, as well as to Europe's role as a global player. It is crucial for Eastern European countries to show that they can provide added value in all these areas (and others) at a time when the 'old' EU member states often see them as a drain on resources. This perception is largely false: if nothing else, Eastern Europe is a vast new market for consumer goods from the EU-10 countries, a source of relatively cheap and well-trained labour and a welcoming destination for foreign investments. What is true, however, is that too often the newly-emerged democracies in Central and Eastern Europe rely too much on Brussels or look for guardian angels among the EU-15; too often they forget that an EU member state is an interesting partner only insofar as it is itself a strong, assertive, economically viable, politically stable and efficient, liberal and tolerant country. Above all, they must create opportunities for their own people at home.

In the meantime, we will need to change the textbooks too. Many of the history and geography books, as well as tourist guides, still appear very much the same as if they had been printed during the Cold War. There, Eastern Europe still seems to be a different and odd place. Above all, we need to build a new, collective history, shared memories and myths, which include the experience of Eastern Europeans in the last fifty or sixty years, in particular the experience of violation of human rights and isolation that Communism brought upon their nations. We also need to include in the curriculum the diversity of the new nations and the ethnic groups in the new Europe, their arts and popular culture, and their tourist sights too. We need to rediscover Slavic Europe (and the other European 'tribes' of the Eastern half of the continent). In foreign policy, we need to include their security concerns, their view of the world and their vision of Europe.

In 1945, Communism forced Ljubo, Karl and many other Eastern Europeans to seek shelter in Western Europe. At that time, they did not realise they were leaving behind 'Eastern Europe'. There was no such thing then. Rather, they felt that their own country had been overtaken by an alien ideology that was so opposed to everything they knew from before that life became unbearable. These were Karl's words exactly: he could not stand the Communist regime's uniformity, which was so alien to him. This new ideology was (literally) after their lives – Ljubo Sirc was sentenced to death, a fate he only narrowly escaped. Many others who stayed at home felt much the same, if not perhaps so intensely. There were so many that did not have the means, the opportunity or simply the courage to leave, but few of them were comfortable with the new system. It was certainly not something that they, by the mere fact of being Eastern Europeans, could put up with.

Today it is freedom of movement – and the continuing lack of economic opportunities at home – that is driving Eastern Europeans away. The Eastern Europeans of 1945 were leaving behind societies that were not that different or distant from the ones they wanted to enter. Since 1990, Eastern Europeans have been moving out of societies that have only just begun to emerge from the gloom of half a century of Communism. But the two halves of Europe have begun to come together, and not only through consumerism (which often takes wild forms in the new member states). In the long-term perspective, the Cold War that kept the two Europes apart for fifty years should soon become relatively unimportant, a short episode in the 2,000 years

158

of European history. Eastern Europeans should be accepted as 'normal' Europeans. The entry at the end of 2007 of the eight new member states into the common travel area created by the Schengen Agreement may work towards this end, if the resulting visitors and migrants are not seen as a threat. Imagine that you can suddenly walk freely through the fields and into another country where, eighteen years earlier, there was still barbed wire, watchtowers and booby-traps, and where people like Karl and Ljubo once escaped across a border under the cover of the night. But not only that: cross-border EU projects and business interests also travel fast. In the Slovenian hinterland of Trieste/Trst, which has featured so prominently in this book, local restaurants are even fuller of Italian guests, who are increasingly buying holiday properties, pushing prices up. As a result, some people from Nova Gorica are buying flats in Gorizia/Gorica. Trieste/Trst is busy thinking how it can now, at last, create a real hinterland in south-east Slovenia and compete with Ljubljana[78].

After all, what is Eastern Europe really? Yes, these are largely Slavic lands, but they are not exclusively so. Greeks, Finns, Albanians, Romanians, Estonians, Latvians and Lithuanians are not Slavs. Yes, these are mostly the lands in which Russia historically played a very significant role, but Finland was the first European country to be at war with the Soviet Union. By contrast, there was never a Russian military presence in Slovenia. Yes, these are lands to the East, but Prague and Ljubljana lie to the west of Helsinki or Stockholm or Vienna. Yes, these are the lands of the former Communist bloc, but totalitarian or autocratic systems also existed in twentieth-century Spain, Portugal and Greece[79]. Even economically speaking, the above average growth

---

[78] But there are less healthy developments as well: the right-wing in Friuli-Venezia Giulia would like armed guards and possibly the army back on the border, to protect them from the real and imagined threats of Eastern Europe.

[79] These countries were once looked upon with scorn: PIGS was an acronym that was used informally by some English-speaking EU diplomats for the group of countries comprising Portugal, Ireland, Greece and Spain. Not any more.

rates in Eastern Europe could, in the long term, enable the East to catch the West. Some of the new member states already boast a GDP per capita higher than that of some of the poorer members of the EU-15.

Eastern Europe was created as a cultural concept in the eighteenth century. Even at that stage, this concept was largely applied to lands under Ottoman rule and only to a lesser extent to those under Russian rule or influence. It was not meant to apply to German-influenced Central Europe. But even that idea of Eastern Europe was ill-informed, based on prejudices and a consequence of philosophical debate at the time in Western Europe, rather than on an objective observation of Eastern Europe. It was only after World War II, with the advent of Communism and the erection of the Berlin Wall, that the current concept of Eastern Europe emerged – a political one, which has, over the years, grown once again into a cultural one. We still have tourist guidebooks to Eastern Europe, well-known consumer brands sell Eastern European versions of their products, GPS devices come with or without Eastern Europe, there is supposedly an Eastern European art, etc. But this book has been aiming to show that, once we look closer at it, Eastern Europe as a cultural concept becomes highly elusive. Indeed, one begins to question whether there has ever been such a thing as Eastern Europe at all. We can only hope that Eastern Europe as a political, social and cultural construct – built on the foundations of the Berlin Wall and past prejudices – is disappearing in front of our eyes.

Further enlargement of the EU should encompass the Balkans, 'Eastern Europe proper' and Turkey, and should one day bring about a whole new dimension to the debate about Eastern Europe. That is, of course, if the enlargement process ever travels further east than Croatia, and recent developments have cast doubt over this. (Can the application by Iceland bring some fresh air into the enlargement debate?) It will be interesting to see whether such enlargement, if it takes place, will shift the concept of 'the East' further eastward or

160

simply enlarge it. Perhaps even more importantly, will Europe ever give up the need to have an East?

Bibliography

Throughout this book there are numerous references to a variety of literature I have used. Here I only list those sources that have been extensively used in the writing or which I consider particularly relevant, or those that I have found especially inspiring.

For a detailed account of the Christianisation of Europe, including Central Europe, see Richard Fletcher, *The Barbarian Conversion: From Paganism to Christianity* (New York, 1997). The last days of the (Western) Roman Empire are examined (with great sympathy towards the Romans) in Bryan Ward-Perkins, *The Fall of Rome and the End of Civilisation* (Oxford, 2005), which also gives an interesting explanation of why the Western empire disappeared, while the Eastern one carried on. An equally sympathetic account of the Byzantine Empire can be found in Warren Treadgold, *A Concise History of Byzantium* (Palgrave, 2001) or in Averil Cameron *The Byzantines* (Blackwell, 2), which I particularly recommend. In his highly readable *Byzantine Christianity – Emperor, Church and the West* (Detroit, 1982) Harry J. Magoulias deals with the religious aspects of Byzantine Christianity and its relationship with the West. *The Myth of Nations – The Medieval Origins of Europe* (Princeton, 2002) is a very provocative reading of the myths about the early formation of the European nations, written by Patrick J. Geary. It leaves all kinds of nationalism, both big and small, looking a bit silly. The general idea of Europe is studied from a number of perspectives in *The Idea of Europe – From Antiquity to the European Union* (Woodrow Wilson Centre, 2002), edited by Anthony Pagden, as well as in Robert Bartlett, *The Making of Europe – Conquest, Colonisation and Cultural Change 950–1350* (Penguin, 1994). A brilliant book on the subject of Europe is Michael Heffernan's *The Meaning of Europe, Geography and Geopolitics* (Arnold, 1998), where the geographic aspect is particularly strong and fascinating. JHH Weiler defends Europe's Christian roots in *Un' Europa cristiana* (BURsaggi, 2003).

Maria Todorova's. *Imagining the Balkans* (Oxford University Press, 1997) is a rather academic, but very thorough and well-argued critical account of stereotypes about the Balkans. The interaction between Islam and Europe is the subject of another book by Richard Fletcher, *The Cross and the Crescent – Christianity and Islam from Muhammad to the Reformation* (Penguin, 2003).

Paula Sutter Fichtner complements a historical account of the Austrian Empire with social and cultural comments in *The Habsburg Monarchy, 149 –1848* (Palgrave Macmillan, 2003). The emergence of Germany is described in Harold James, *A German Identity* (London, 2000). Friedrich Naumann's *Central Europe* (New York, 1917) is now of great historic curiosity only (and only available through rare bookshops). The post-World War I years are brilliantly described in Margaret MacMillan's highly readable *Peacemakers – The Paris Conference of 1919 and Its Attempt to End War* (London, 2001), which is of great help in understanding why Europe went to war once again in 1939. A similarly excellent account of the civilisation of the entire continent is Eric von Kuehnelt-Leddihn's *The Intelligent American's Guide to Europe* (Arlington House, 1979), also a must-read for every intelligent European trying to understand European history. It is probably the best book I have ever read about European civilisation. More conventional, but still very readable, is JM Roberts' *History of Europe* (Penguin, 1997).

My main source for the general history of Central Europe (although limited to the history of the Czech lands, Slovakia, Poland and Hungary) was Piotr S. Wandycz, *The Price of Freedom, A History of East Central Europe from the Middle Ages to the Present* (Routledge, 2001). *The Palgrave Concise Historical Atlas of Eastern Europe* (Palgrave, 2001) by Dennis P. Hupchick and Harold E. Cox was an excellent companion, as were the 'official' histories found on the government web pages of the countries concerned. Adrian Hyde-Price's *The International Politics of East Central Europe* (Manchester University Press, 1996) has a very valuable overview of bilateral relations in the region. Most of the economic data and observations in this book are based on *The Origins of Backwardness in Eastern Europe* (University of California Press, 1991) by Daniel Chirot (ed.), and Angus Maddison's *The World Economy: Historical Statistics* (OECD 2003). The latter presents the backbone of the economic arguments in my book, while the social and cultural aspects are in great part based on *Inventing Eastern Europe* (Stanford University Press, 1994) by Larry Wolff, which is a detailed study of the emergence of the concept of Eastern Europe, also with examples from literature.

A very good source of documents about the Cold War period is Martin McCauley's excellent *The Origins of the Cold War 1941–1949* (Pearson Longman, 2003). Events since the 1970s are the subject of Bülent Gökay's *Eastern Europe since 1970* (Longman, Pearson 2001). The modern geopolitical challenges in Eastern Europe are the subject of Ola Tunander et al (ed.), *Geopolitics in Post-wall Europe – Security, Territory and Identity* (PRIO, Sage, 1997) and Andrew H. Dawson and Rick Fawn (eds.), *The Changing Geopolitics of Eastern Europe* (Frank Cass, 2002).

Finally, two more recent books can be recommended: Tony Judt's *Post-war* (William Heinemann: London, 2005), which is not only an excellent social, political and cultural history of Europe, but also pays a great deal of attention to the developments in Eastern Europe, and Norman Davies' *Europe East & West* (Jonathan Cape, London, 2006), which deals with the historical aspects of this book in more detail.

Index